IMPRESSIONS of home™
HOMES DESIGNED WITH THE LOOK YOU WANT

EDITOR	Bruce Arant
PLANS EDITOR	Tina Leyden
GRAPHIC DESIGNERS	Yen Gutowski
	Heather Guthrie
	Oanh Heiser
ILLUSTRATOR	Heather Guthrie
RENDERING COLORIZATION	Alva Louden
	Beth Davis
RENDERING ILLUSTRATORS	Shawn Doherty
	Silvia Boyd
	Perry Gauthier
	George McDonald, dec.
TECHNICAL ADVISER	Rob Phillips
PUBLICATIONS ASSISTANT	Lori Walling
CIRCULATION MANAGER	Priscilla Ivey
PUBLISHER	Dennis Brozak
ASSOCIATE PUBLISHER	Linda Reimer

IMPRESSIONS of home™
HOMES DESIGNED WITH THE LOOK YOU WANT

IS PUBLISHED BY:
Design Basics Publications
11112 John Galt Blvd., Omaha, NE 68137
Web – www.designbasics.com
E-Mail – info@designbasics.com

CHIEF EXECUTIVE OFFICER	Dennis Brozak
PRESIDENT	Linda Reimer
DIRECTOR OF MARKETING	Kevin Blair
BUSINESS DEVELOPMENT	Paul Foresman
CONTROLLER	Janie Murnane
EDITOR IN CHIEF	Bruce Arant

COVER PHOTO: Plan #48A-1855 Bennington
As seen on page 84

BUILDER: Focus Homes, Inc.

HOME PLAN DESIGN SERVICE

LIBRARY OF CONGRESS NUMBER: 99-072437
ISBN: 1-892150-11-5

the Look You Want

Our views and impressions of home are singular to be sure. When we casually pass by homes in a neighborhood, we meet each one with a different emotion. They speak to us selectively. And it is often among these, that we find one we would choose for ourselves. Perhaps it is something in its design, its style, its overall makeup or the way in which its windows are paired. It's as though when we look at it, someone designed it for us. It's not for everyone, we know. Maybe that is why we are more than sure it is for us.

When most of us imagine home in our minds, what we most certainly see first is its exterior. This view encapsulates it, often setting the tone and atmosphere of its presence. While a home is much more than its elevation, its look and style are still, undoubtedly important. Its exterior is an introduction to all. Therefore, it must be significant. And for each of us, it should say something about who we are.

No matter what look defines us, or how we go about discovering that look, IMPRESSIONS of home™ - Homes Designed With The Look You Want, was developed to help you find the right style and character for your home. Inside, 19 design "trios" are showcased featuring three unique elevation styles so you can be sure that what characterizes you, will not have to be sacrificed for your floor plan needs. Insight into each of these design trios is offered from either the designers who created the floor plans or homeowners who've lived in them. These unique perspectives reveal all the more reason the home you build should be your individual expression. IMPRESSIONS of home™ was designed to aid you in your search and eventual discovery.

A. Canton

#48A-5035 S *Price Code* A15

ONE CONCEPT...

One of the greatest assets of this floor plan is its efficiency. In each of the three designs there is very little wasted space, which makes it a great home for buyers who don't need a lot of extra room, such as, an empty-nest couple, a young family or single individuals. When you walk in, the great room automatically catches your eye as it centers on the fireplace. It's a great feature to draw you into the home.

3 LOOKS...

All of the elevations, though traditional, offer their own unique style through individual combinations of brick and siding and different treatments to the roofline. The floor plans are very similar in nature, with a few options to choose from.

A. The Canton (at left) offers a two bedroom option with a more elaborate master bath, as well as a private porch.

B. In the Winter Woods (pg. 4) extra roominess was provided in the garage, as well as tall windows in the great room.

C. The Aspen (pg. 5) also features a covered area to finish into a retreat, located next to the kitchen.

A second window and elongated snack bar are additional features in this breakfast area.

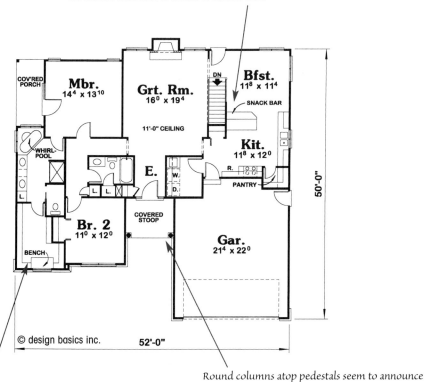

© design basics inc.   52'-0"

Round columns atop pedestals seem to announce the recessed covered stoop on this entry.

beautiful window will add openness to
large walk-in closet. The bench is perfect
resting to put on one's shoes or deciding on
utfit for the day!

1552 Finished SQ. FT.

NOTE: 9 ft. main level walls

B. Winter Woods

#48A-8091 S *Price Code* A13

The tall transoms in the great room help create a
long view from the entry through the great room.

The snack bar in this kitchen is an ideal
buffet counter when serving guests.

The large walk-in closet provides
plenty of room for him and her.

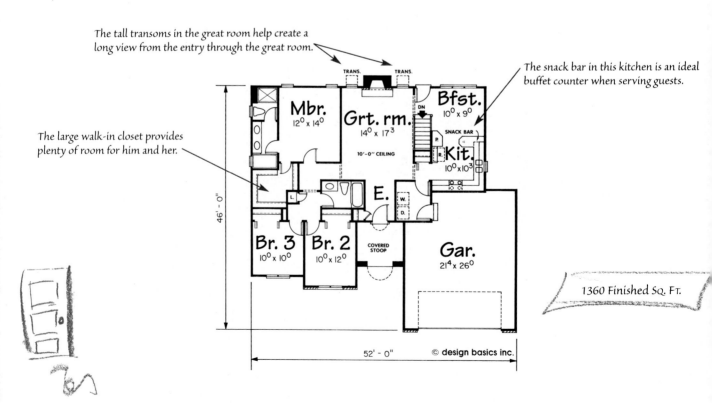

Mbr.
12⁰ x 14⁰

Grt. rm.
14⁰ x 17³

10'-0" CEILING

TRANS. TRANS.

Bfst.
10⁰ x 9⁰

SNACK BAR

Kit.
10⁰ x 10³

E.

Br. 3
10⁰ x 10⁰

Br. 2
10⁰ x 12⁰

COVERED
STOOP

Gar.
21⁴ x 26⁰

46' - 0"

52' - 0"

© design basics inc.

1360 Finished Sq. Ft.

C. Aspen

#48A-3102 S *Price Code* A13

A volume ceiling in the great room prevents this design (and each of the others) from feeling enclosed.

Developing the side, covered area into a porch would be a welcome retreat for this home.

xtra storage space in the garage means om is available for a workbench.

1339 Finished Sq. Ft.

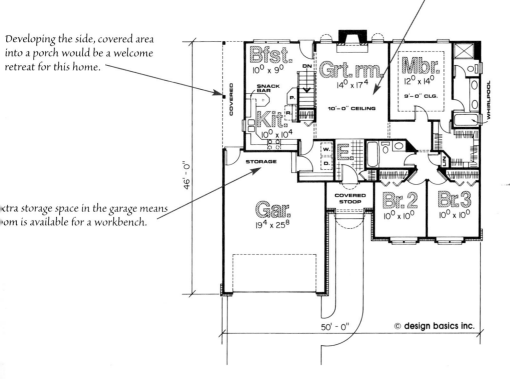

Bfst. 10⁰ x 9⁰

SNACK BAR

Kit. 10⁰ x 10⁴

COVERED

DN

P.

R.

Grt. rm. 14⁰ x 17⁴

10'-0" CEILING

Mbr. 12⁰ x 14⁰

9'-0" CLG.

WHIRLPOOL

W. D.

LIN

STORAGE

Gar. 19⁴ x 25⁸

COVERED STOOP

Br. 2 10⁰ x 10⁰

Br. 3 10⁰ x 10⁰

46'-0"

50'-0"

© design basics inc.

HOME OWNER IMPRESSIONS
ON LIVING IN THE SINCLAIR

There comes a stage in everyone's life when it's time to take care of oneself. To indulge oneself. To pay attention to ones own needs. For Crystal and Gary, the time had come. Their children were grown and ready to start college. Gary had started a new job, and they both felt it was time for them to look for a new home. Now was the time to think about what they wanted.

Gary thought about his need for a home office, since he would be working out of their home. Crystal thought about her desire for the tall ceilings she loved in the homes she'd lived in in the past. She thought about her desire for a large master suite. And they both thought about their favorite pastime - golf.

The day they set foot in Design Basics' Sinclair, it felt like a natural fit. As they toured the home, everything just seemed to fall into place - each space, somehow just right for them. They were close to a golf course where they could fully enjoy their days on the green. There was office space for Gary and even for Crystal, who'd acquired a library of books over the years as a reading teacher. There was no formal living room - a room they'd rarely used in their previous home - only the wide open space of a great room. "It was just kind of immediate," Crystal says. "Right when you walked in there was the expanse of the entry and the openness of the dining room and great room. It just made the whole home feel open."

There was the luxury of the master suite, with a large walk in closet and plenty of room in the bath to get dressed in the morning. It was separate from the other bedrooms - they both wanted that privacy.

1911 Finished SQ. FT.

A den with double doors that open into the great room may replace this bedroom.

It's important that bathrooms be well lit. Here, skylights offer that feature in both the main and master.

continued on page 8

IMPRESSIONS- *Homes designed with the look you wan*

A. Sinclair

#48A-1748 S *Price Code A19*

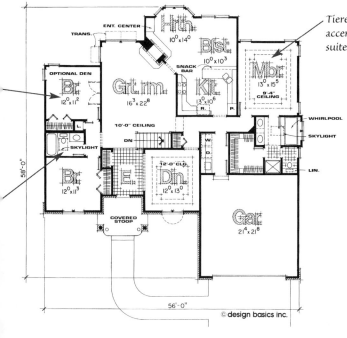

Tiered ceilings are great accents in the master suite and dining room.

(Floor plan labels)

ENT. CENTER
TRANS.
Hrth
10⁰x14⁰
Bfst
10⁰x10³
OPTIONAL DEN
Br
12⁰x11²
Gr.t.rm.
16³x22⁸
SNACK BAR
Kit
13⁰x10⁶
Mbr
13⁰x15⁵
8'-4" CEILING
WHIRLPOOL
SKYLIGHT
L.
10'-0" CEILING
R.
P.
SKYLIGHT
DN
W.
D.
12'-0" CLG.
Din
12⁰x13⁰
LIN.
Br
12⁰x11³
E.
58'-0"
COVERED STOOP
Gar
21⁴x21⁸
56'-0"
© design basics inc.

ONE CONCEPT...

One of the most-liked features of this design is the separation of the master suite from the secondary bedrooms. This provides ideal privacy for older children or guests. While many plans can offer this sought-after feature, the uniqueness of this design lies in the appealing angle of its fireplace, which offers beauty in the great room and seems to naturally create a relaxed, everyday area to unwind between the kitchen, breakfast area and hearth room. The kitchen is in a deliberate, centralized location, so that it is just steps from the garage and the dining room.

3 LOOKS...

The exterior design of these homes has a wide range of appeal, fitting for a variety of neighborhoods and personal preference.

A. The Sinclair (at left) uses more traditional elements, such as brick and smooth arches for a crisp, traditional look that will get noticed.

B. The Enfield (pg. 8) has classic features, such as shutters and Doric columns, that add timelessness to its facade.

C. Stone creates the rustic allure of the Hunter's Crossing (pg. 9). A casual front porch and framed entry only add to the home's attraction.

For Crystal and Gary, the Sinclair lives as efficiently as an apartment, but allows them room for family and guests if they drop in. "One of the reasons we like this home, is that everything is just right here. And when the kids come home or Gary goes into the office, they can go to the other end of the house. We like that separation," Crystal says.

Even though the home seemed to meet their needs almost immediately, Gary and Crystal were still not sure about the hearth room. It was not large enough for much furniture and not integrated with any one area. They first thought they would much rather have had that space devoted to the great room, where they anticipated spending more of their time.

But after placing a couple of chairs, a footstool and table there, they came to find it a favorite spot to read in the evenings. "Now, I don't think a day goes by

where we don't use the hearth room," Crystal says.

Another favorite pastime for Crystal and Gary, was to visit open houses on the weekends. They looked, Gary says, always searching to find something out there that they might want in the future. Now, that pastime has all but been abandoned. "I think we both feel like we've arrived at a home that's really meant for us," Gary says. "It's a safe place. It's a place where we both just enjoy being.

B. Enfield

#48A- 5141 S *Price Code* A22

The built-in desk was undoubtedly designed as a study area for a child.

The expanded hearth room in this version enjoys proximity to the fireplace as well as views out its bayed windows.

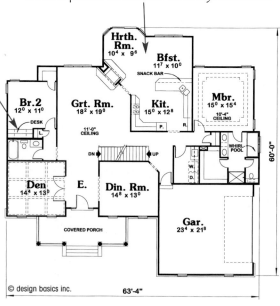

Unfinished Attic adds 613 Sq. Ft.

The option of an attic adds versatility to this design. An extra bedroom or hobby room would be great uses for this space.

2242 Finished Sq. Ft.

NOTE: 9 ft. main level walls

IMPRESSIONS- *Homes designed with the look you wan*

C. Hunters Crossing

#48A-8019 S *Price Code* A19

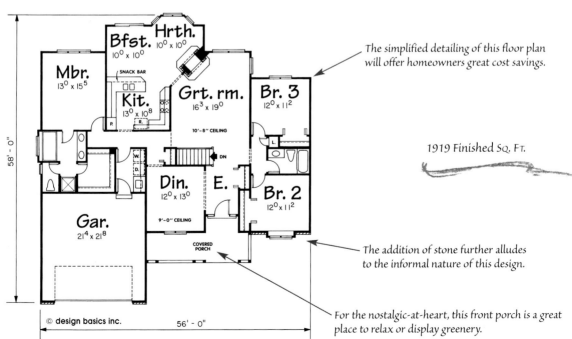

The simplified detailing of this floor plan will offer homeowners great cost savings.

1919 Finished Sq. Ft.

The addition of stone further alludes to the informal nature of this design.

For the nostalgic-at-heart, this front porch is a great place to relax or display greenery.

#48A-2318 S *Price Code* A35

Rockford

#48A-2127 S *Price Code* A22

Montrose

The kitchen is offered the utility of a walk-in pantry and island counter, and the coziness of a hearth room.

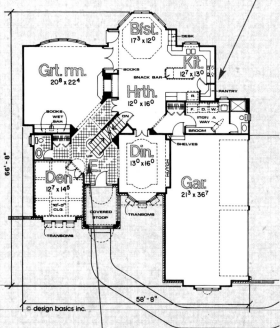

The diagonal stairway defines the interesting shapes and angles of the great room, master suite and den.

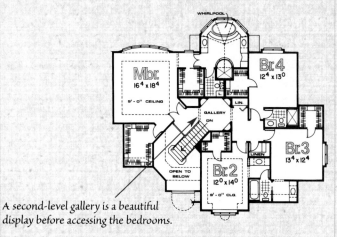

A second-level gallery is a beautiful display before accessing the bedrooms.

Main: 1871 Sq. Ft.
Second: 1677 Sq. Ft.

Total: 3548 Sq. Ft.

The living and family rooms connect through a set of French doors, which also give privacy to each area.

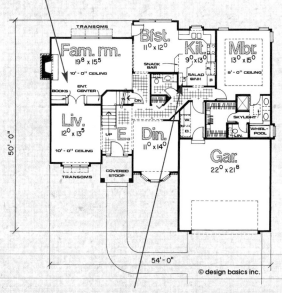

In the kitchen, a highly functional peninsula island offers extra counter space and a salad sink.

A second-level clothes chute makes laundry a less arduous chore in this home.

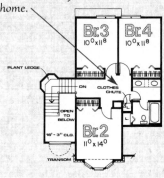

Main: 1602 Sq. Ft.
Second: 654 Sq. Ft.

Total: 2256 Sq. Ft.

IMPRESSIONS- *Homes designed with the look you wan*

#48A-1867 S *Price Code* A19

Langley

#48A-3196 S *Price Code* A21

Galloway

This screen porch is a great place for fresh air and a relaxing view.

The living room can access the family room, if entertaining a large group.

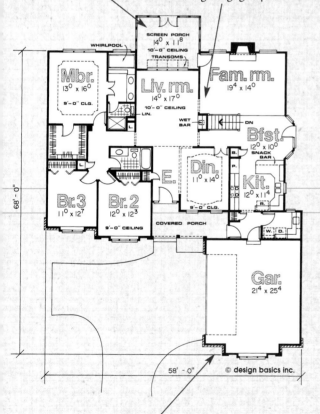

This interior side-load garage creates a clean frontal view of the home.

2120 Finished Sq. Ft.

The dining room is in an excellent location within this home. It is integrated with the great room when entertaining and, when not in use, it makes a wonderful vista.

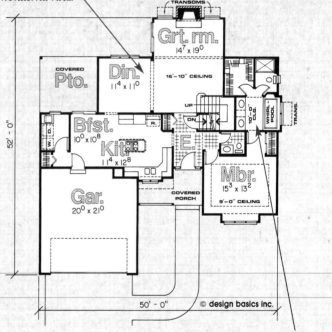

A tall window and 10-foot ceiling really gives the master bath added dimension and openness.

The staircase is a wonderful element in this home. It wraps around to the second level where a cat-walk views the entry and great room.

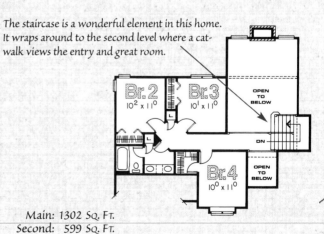

Main: 1302 Sq. Ft.
Second: 599 Sq. Ft.

Total: 1901 Sq. Ft.

Design Trio #3

A. The Jefferson
B. The Adams Creek
C. The Branford

One Concept...

The entry in this design calls attention to two areas in this home. The stairway is one of those areas. It's U-shape makes it pop out right as you walk in. You actually have to walk past the stairway and come back to access the second level. It is a very effective visual tool in the entry. Adjoining the entry is a large living area with the fireplace as the main feature when you walk in. It is very large and open, so you really feel like it draws you into it.

3 Looks...

A. The Jefferson (at right) really has a pleasant elevation with a large arched window on the second level catching your eye. The porch really gives it more of a country feel.

B. The bare bones, essential aspects of the Jefferson can be found in the Adams Creek (pg. 13). Though simplified, it still has a great deal of presence through its substantial porch columns and brick detail on the garage.

C. The Branford (pg. 14) definitely has an established feel to it. It's vertical massing is reminiscent of homes built on narrow city lots. The brick siding and double-hung windows seem to complete this effect.

A. Jefferson

#48A-2890 S   *Price Code* A17

This island counter with large snack bar creates a natural buffet counter or extra space for seating guests.

A wide make-up counter in the master bath is a great extra feature when getting ready.

Built-in bookshelves in the living room are ideal for displaying family momentos.

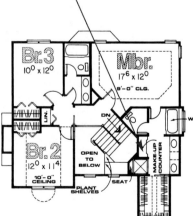

Main: 884 SQ. FT.
Second: 848 SQ. FT.

Total: 1732 SQ. FT.

IMPRESSIONS- *Homes designed with the look you wan*

B. *Adams Creek*

#48A-8105 S *Price Code* A16

Main: 910 Sq. Ft.
Second: 775 Sq. Ft.

Total: 1685 Sq. Ft.

An angled snack bar adds definition to the kitchen and creates a secondary eating area.

Shared space between the great and dining rooms makes it easy to entertain guests.

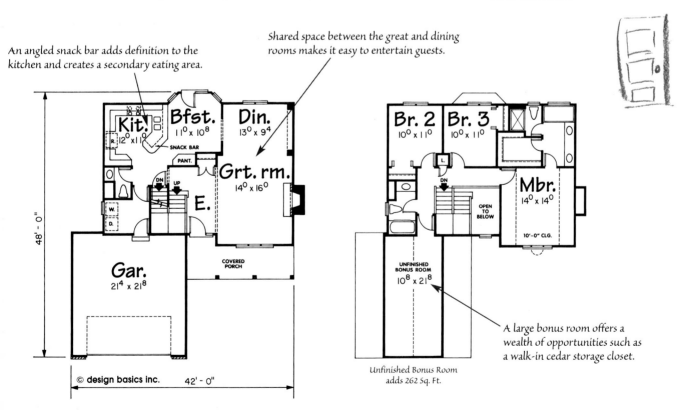

Kit. R.: 12⁰ x 11⁰

SNACK BAR

Bfst. 11⁰ x 10⁸

PANT.

Din. 13⁰ x 9⁴

Grt. rm. 14⁰ x 16⁰

DN UP

E.

W. D.

Gar. 21⁴ x 21⁸

COVERED PORCH

48' - 0"

© design basics inc.   42' - 0"

Br. 2 10⁰ x 11⁰

Br. 3 10⁰ x 11⁰

L

DN

Mbr. 14⁰ x 14⁰

OPEN TO BELOW

10'-0" CLG.

UNFINISHED BONUS ROOM 10⁸ x 21⁸

A large bonus room offers a wealth of opportunities such as a walk-in cedar storage closet.

Unfinished Bonus Room adds 262 Sq. Ft.

C. Branford

#48A-5085 S *Price Code* A19

A built-in bookcase and see-through fireplace create warmth in this everyday hearth room.

The dressing area in the master bath makes sense between a walk-in closet and dual-sink vanity.

51'-0"

Kit.
12⁰ x 12⁰

Bfst.
11⁰ x 11⁸

Hrth.
Rm.
14⁰ x 12⁰

SNACK BAR

BOOKS

P.

DN   UP

E.

BOOKS

W.
D.

Liv.
Rm.
14⁰ x 16⁰

STOOP

Gar.
24⁴ x 23⁸

46'-0"   © design basics inc.

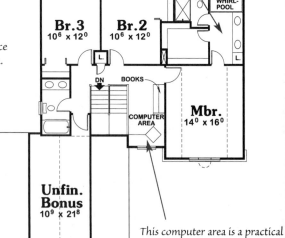

Br.3
10⁶ x 12⁰

Br.2
10⁶ x 12⁰

WHIRL-
POOL

L.

DN   BOOKS

L.

COMPUTER
AREA

Mbr.
14⁰ x 16⁰

Unfin.
Bonus
10⁹ x 21⁸

This computer area is a practical place to do homework or finish office work.

Unfinished Bonus Room
adds 262 Sq. Ft.

Main: 1002 Sq. Ft.
Second: 926 Sq. Ft.

Total: 1928 Sq. Ft.

NOTE: 9 ft. main level walls

IMPRESSIONS- *Homes designed with the look you wa*

A. Cyprus

#48A-2648 S *Price Code A19*

Built-in bookshelves in the family room are a great idea for TV and electronic equipment.

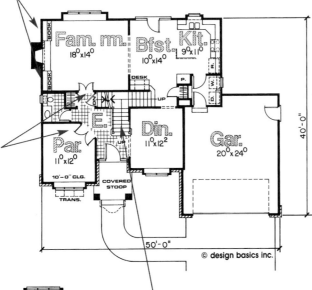

 french doors add beauty to the parlor and family room while allowing each space to be private.

© design basics inc.

A T-shaped stairway allows two access points to the second floor and provides further segregation between formal and informal areas.

Main: 1082 Sq. Ft.
Second: 869 Sq. Ft.

Total: 1951 Sq. Ft.

One Concept...

One of the basic elements of this floor plan is its family activity area that's separated from the entry. This is a great feature for families with children, who will use the area on a daily basis and cannot always keep it neat. A second element of this floor plan is the fact that it has a second living area on the main floor. This is an area where buyers can go just to get away, or where they can entertain guests. The master suite in this home also features a large walk-in closet, which is an amenity that homebuyers really seem to appreciate.

3 Looks...

A. The elevation of the Cyprus (at left) has a little bit more of a contemporary flair with the roofline creating long, proportionately slanted lines.

B. There are definitely more windows on the elevation of the Linden (pg. 16) than the Cyprus, because we decided to go with a very traditional style. And since this home has a fourth bedroom, the tall massing on the left side of the home seemed to call for it.

C. The elevation of the Hazelwood (pg. 17), is again a traditional style, but it has a more established feel which was accomplished primarily by our use of brick and the controlled size of the windows. The windows do not look out of proportion on this elevation, but because they are not the dominating feature, it brings back the feeling of older homes, which did not typically feature large windows.

B. Linden

#48A-2638 S *Price Code A21*

An island counter makes this kitchen feel more open, and provides accessible counter space for cooking.

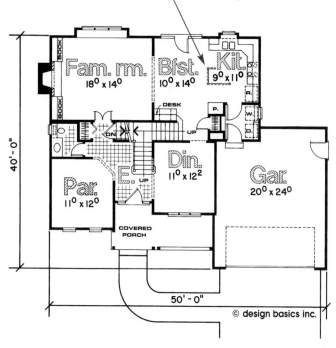

40'-0"

Fam. rm. 18⁰ x 14⁰
Bfst. 10⁰ x 14⁰
Kit. 9⁰ x 11⁰
BOOK
BOOK
DESK
P.
R.
W.
D.
UP
DN
Par. 11⁰ x 12⁰
E. UP
Din. 11⁰ x 12²
Gar. 20⁰ x 24⁰
COVERED PORCH

50'-0"

© design basics inc.

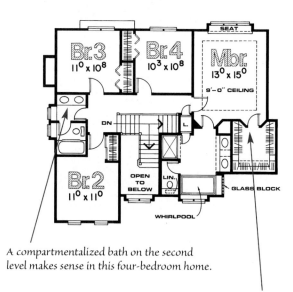

Br.3 11⁰ x 10⁸
Br.4 10³ x 10⁸
Mbr. 13⁰ x 15⁰
9'-0" CEILING
SEAT
DN
L
Br.2 11⁰ x 11⁰
OPEN TO BELOW
LIN.
WHIRLPOOL
GLASS BLOCK

A compartmentalized bath on the second level makes sense in this four-bedroom home.

Buyers will appreciate the subtle details in this mast suite: a window seat, natural light above the whirlp tub and an indented entry to the walk-in closet tha perfect for a three-way mirror.

Main: 1082 SQ. FT.
Second: 1021 SQ. FT.

Total: 2103 SQ. FT.

C. Hazelwood

#48A-5504 S *Price Code* **A25**

A large walk-in pantry offers storage space to the kitchen.

Surrounded in glass, this sunroom will be a favorite place to relax or entertain.

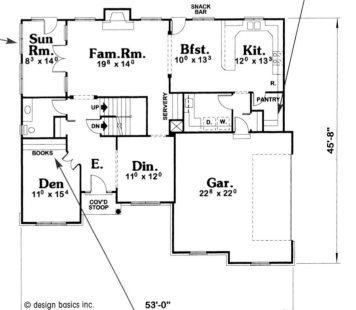

Main: 1390 SQ. FT.
Second: 1129 SQ. FT.

Total: 2519 SQ. FT.

NOTE: 9 ft. main level walls

A built-in bookshelf, which takes up a complete wall, will be a great focal point in this den.

design basics inc.
HOME PLAN DESIGN SERVICE

ORDER DIRECT- (800) 947-7526   **17**

Gainsborough

The family room is anything but traditional with built-in entertainment center, bookshelves and stunning windows that stretch to the ceiling.

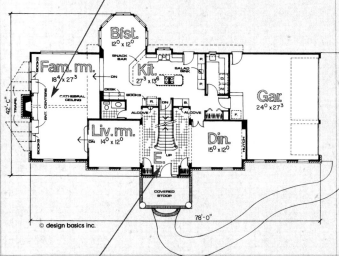

- Bfst. 12⁰ x 12⁰
- Fam. rm. 18⁴ x 27³
- Kit. 27³ x 13⁶
- Gar. 24⁰ x 27³
- Liv. rm. 14⁰ x 12⁰
- Din. 15⁰ x 12⁰

© design basics inc.
78'-0"

A traditional entry, with central stairway and formal rooms to each side, suits the Southern Colonial styling of its exterior.

The sloped ceiling and window seat in bedroom 4 makes a quaint area a child will enjoy.

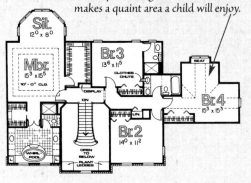

- Sit. 12⁰ x 8⁰
- Mbr. 15³ x 15⁵
- Br 3 13⁶ x 11⁵
- Br 4 15³ x 15³
- Br. 2 14⁰ x 11²

Main: 1717 Sq. Ft.
Second: 1518 Sq. Ft.

Total: 3235 Sq. Ft.

Stanton Showcase

Separate vanities and walk-in closets are exceptional features in this master suite.

This open veranda is truly useable space because of its accessibility from family room and kitchen.

- CLO 9' CH
- BREAKFAST 11'-0" x 10'-0" 9' CH
- VERANDA
- SHWR
- MASTER BEDROOM 13'-0" x 18'-0" 10'-12' CH
- MASTR BATH 9' CH
- 2 STORY FAMILY ROOM 17'-0" x 15'-0" 18' CH
- KITCHEN 11'-0" x 15'-0" 9' CH
- CLO 9' CH
- UTIL. 9' CH
- W D
- PNTRY
- STORAGE 9' CH
- POWDER 9' CH
- COAT CLO
- ENTRY 9' CH
- DINING ROOM 11'-0" x 13'-6" 9' CH
- GARAGE 9' CH
- PORCH
- STUDY 11'-0" x 13'-0" 9' CH

56'-10"
65'-6"

© CARMICHAEL & DAME DESIGNS, INC.

The study will be used as much for personal enjoyment as a place for work.

- BEDROOM 4 11'-0" x 15'-0" 8'-10' CH
- 2 STORY FAMILY ROOM 17'-0" x 15'-0" 18' CH
- BATH 3 8' CH
- 324 sq. ft. OPTIONAL ATTIC
- BDRM 3 11'-0" x 12'-0" 8'-10' CH
- BEDROOM 2 11'-0" x 13'-0" 8'-10' CH

Main: 1844 Sq. Ft.
Second: 794 Sq. Ft.

Total: 2638 Sq. Ft.

Slab and Basement Foundation Plans Included.

IMPRESSIONS– *Homes designed with the look you want*

Dunhill Manor

#48A-9168 S *Price Code* B29

The stairhall will be a great place to mingle with a view of this central see-through fireplace.

The kitchen is set at an angle which provides both interest as well as integration with the breakfast area and living room.

The living room, which is visually stunning when entertaining, also provides the casual feature of built-ins for everyday enjoyment.

Main: 2069 Sq. Ft.
Second: 897 Sq. Ft.

Total: 2966 Sq. Ft.

Slab and Basement Foundation Plans Included.

#48A-24002 S *Price Code* A22

Hanson

The master suite is separated from the three bedrooms, which are near the laundry room and share a compartmented bath.

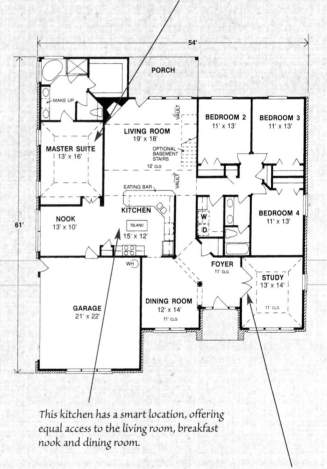

This kitchen has a smart location, offering equal access to the living room, breakfast nook and dining room.

The study has its two necessities - seclusion and access to the front entry (for possible clients).

2250 Finished Sq. Ft.

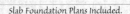

Slab Foundation Plans Included.

---

design basics inc.
HOME PLAN DESIGN SERVICE

DESIGN TRIO #5

A. THE EAGLES RIDGE
B. THE HAWKESBURY
C. THE LAUREN

ONE CONCEPT...

Definitely the advantage of this plan is that it is a larger family-style, one-story floor plan with a family room setting off the kitchen and breakfast area where all of the daily activity can take place. This area will feel like one room because of its openness. The family room is large and features a nice fireplace as a focal point. The kitchen features an island counter with cooking range that creates an even more open atmosphere in which to interact. Buyers also have at least three bedrooms in each design with the option of a fourth, depending on their needs.

3 LOOKS...

A. The Eagles Ridge (at right), has a bit more rustic charm, allowing the choice of stone and shake siding to dictate its overall appeal. This elevation will look stunning in an area with lots of trees and vegetation.

B. The Hawkesbury (pg. 21), has a very distinct elevation with lots of symmetry that is consequently carried through inside the home.

C. Buyers looking for a more straightforward, traditional design may enjoy the appeal of the Lauren (pg. 22), with its use of double gables to draw attention to its windows and entry. This creates the main visual appeal of the elevation.

A. Eagles Ridge

#48A-8023 S   *Price Code A24*

2467 Finished Sq. Ft.

The living and dining rooms make up the central core of the home, an element accentuated by shared open space and ceiling height.

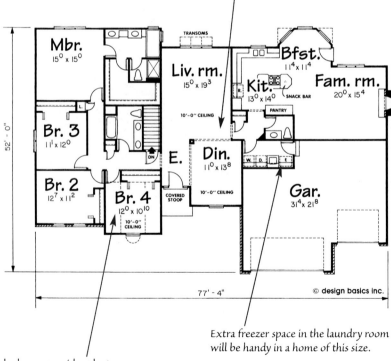

A fourth bedroom provides plenty of room to accommodate a family.

Extra freezer space in the laundry room will be handy in a home of this size.

IMPRESSIONS— *Homes designed with the look you want*

B. Hawkesbury

#48A-2206 S   *Price Code* A24

Built-in bookshelves are a great idea
to enclose TV and stereo equipment.

A compartmentalized bath makes sense,
so that more than one can get ready.

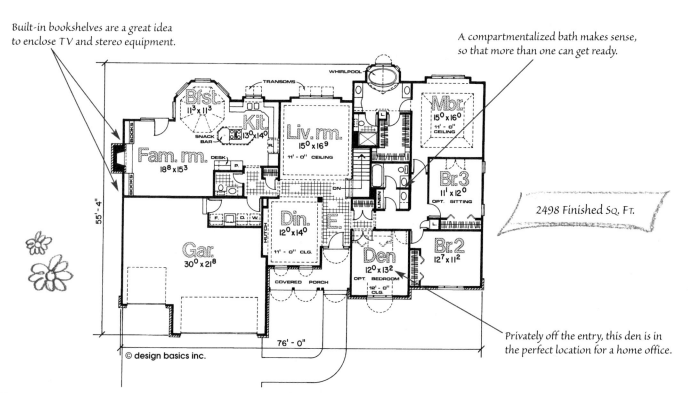

2498 Finished Sq. Ft.

Privately off the entry, this den is in
the perfect location for a home office.

© design basics inc.

C. Lauren

#48A-5513 S *Price Code A26*

A sitting room off the master suite will make a great place for parents to get away.

This quaint porch will be a great place to relax or cook outdoors in nice weather.

Storage space is a great option and provides a place to store tools and a workbench.

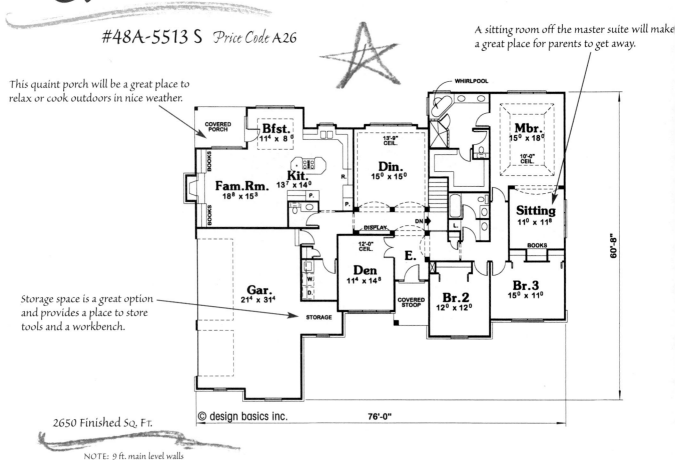

2650 Finished Sq. Ft.

© design basics inc.

76'-0"

60'-8"

NOTE: 9 ft. main level walls

IMPRESSIONS- *Homes designed with the look you wa*

Woodlands Showcase

#48A-9160 S *Price Code* B26

...he back porch is joined by the ...reakfast area and master suite.

This cathedral ceiling which spans the family room and kitchen will bring great visual connection to this area.

Floor plan — Main level:

MASTER BEDROOM 13'-0" X 17'-0" 9' C.H.

PORCH

FP

BREAKFAST 11'-0" X 12'-0" 9' C.H.

MASTER BATH

PWDR

FAMILY ROOM 19'-0" X 15'-0" 17' C.H.

R W D

UTILITY

KITCHEN 13'-4" X 15'-0" 11'-19' C.H.

SERV. ENTRY PANT

MASTER CLOSET

GALLERY 9' C.H.

BUTLER'S

ENTRY 18' C.H.

DINING ROOM 11'-0" X 13'-0" 9' C.H.

DN UP

STUDY 12'-6" X 13'-0" 9' C.H.

PORCH

3-CAR GARAGE 9' C.H.

57'- 1 1/2"

65'-3"

© CARMICHAEL & DAME DESIGNS, INC.

A walk-in pantry can have a variety of uses with its close proximity to the kitchen, as well as the utility area.

The master suite defines luxury, with a sitting area and pair of built-in dressers in the walk-in closet.

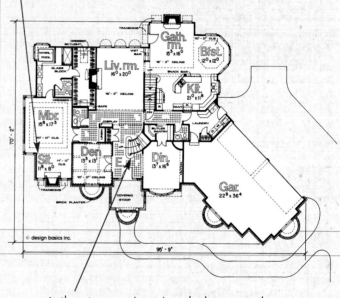

TRANSOMS

WHIRL POOL

GLASS BLOCK

DRESSER

WET BAR

Gath. rm. 15'³ x 16'⁰

10'-0" CLG.

Bfst. 12'⁰ x 12'⁰

Liv. rm. 16'⁰ x 20'⁰ 18'- 3" CEILING

SNACK BAR

Kit. 21'⁰ x 11'⁸

Mbr. 15'⁸ x 17'³

SAFE

DISPLAY

BUTLER PANTRY

PANT.

LAUNDRY

70'- 2"

Sit. 11'⁸ x 8'⁰ 10'-0" CLG.

Den 13' x 13'

E Din. 13'⁷ x 16'⁰

TRANSOMS 10'-0" CEILING

BRICK PLANTER

COVERED STOOP

Gar. 22'⁸ x 36'⁴

© design basics inc.

95'- 9"

In the entry, a curving staircase leads to a second-level balcony with beautiful display shelves.

Floor plan — Second level (Woodlands):

BEDROOM 2 13'-0" X 11'-0" 8' C.H.

W.I.C.

LIN LIN

OPEN TO FAMILY ROOM

OPEN TO KITCHEN

LIN

BATH

DN BALCONY ATTIC

OPEN TO BELOW

BEDROOM 4 11'-0" X 11'-0" 8' C.H.

BEDROOM 3 12'-6" X 11'-0" 8' C.H.

With walk-in closets and private baths, each second-level bedroom becomes its own retreat.

Floor plan — Second level (Churchill):

Br 4 15' x 12'⁰ 9'-0" CEILING

Br 3 14' x 13'⁰ 9'-0" CEILING

DISPLAY AREA

LINEN

OPEN TO BELOW

Br 2 12'⁷ x 17'⁰ 9'-0" CEILING

Main: 1960 SQ. FT.
Second: 749 SQ. FT.

Total: 2655 SQ. FT.

Slab and Basement Foundation Plans Included.

Main: 2839 SQ. FT.
Second: 1111 SQ. FT.

Total: 3950 SQ. FT.

HOME OWNER IMPRESSIONS

ON LIVING IN THE FAYETTE

When Robert crawls out of bed at 5:00 a.m., he heads off to his adjoining master bath where he showers and gets ready for the day, all without ever waking his wife Barbara. To him, that is one of the most important features of his home, Design Basics' Fayette. Ever since Robert and Barbara ventured into the realm of homeownership, they've lived in a two-story. The privacy, the separation, the discriminating design philosophy of segregated living and sleeping has stayed with them their whole lives. And when the time came to build their dream home, no other design style would do. Design Basics Fayette, became their fifth two-story home.

It may seem hard to believe that Robert and Barbara - technically considered "empty-nesters" with two grown children and four grandchildren - would choose a two-story home. But according to Robert, it was the only suitable choice. A manager for a steel mill, Robert rises early to head off to work and subsequently retires to bed at an early hour. Having a quiet atmosphere in which to sleep was a critical element of the home to him.

"First and foremost, home is a sanctuary," Robert says. "I need a place that I can come to at the end of the day and recharge my battery. After looking at many designs, we kept coming back to this one."

Seclusion was not only important on the interior of the home, it was also an important feature of their lot, as well. It was so important, that Robert and Barbara waited

continued on page 26

The living and dining room are married in the elegance of repeating transom windows, boxed ceiling and columns.

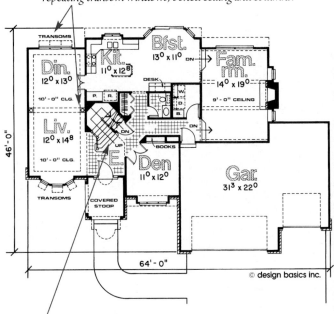

A great memory point in this home is its angled stairway. It makes an impressive statement in the entry.

24

ONE CONCEPT...

Not only was this floor plan designed for a family with the need for four bedrooms, it was also designed for those who desire formal entertaining areas that are separate from the everyday areas of the home. The massive family room is unforgetable in this home and makes a great area for kids to play while adults interact. A compartmentalized bath that is shared by three bedrooms on the second floor, is a key element, allowing more than one chile to get ready.

3 LOOKS...

A. The spaciousness of the Fayette (at left), calls for a dramatic exterior. It is expressed here in a steeply hipped roofline and muntin windows with transoms.

B. The Attleboro (pg. 26) allows its wide windows to be the dominating feature of the elevation. Their double-hung styling is paired with symmetrial arches and classic trim detail.

C. The Stone Creek (pg. 27), is noticeably less adorned, but is still noteworthy for its front porch and tall central massing with stacked windows.

A. Fayette

#48A-2346 S   Price Code A24

The design of the master bath is relaxing in nature with his and her vanities and corner whirlpool with side windows.

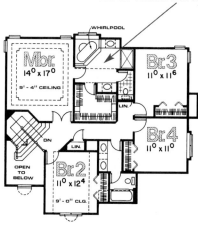

Main: 1369 SQ. FT.
Second: 1111 SQ. FT.

Total: 2480 SQ. FT.

more than five years to build in the highly wooded area where their home now sits.

At over 2,400 square feet, the Fayette features a variety of living areas, which was also important, according to Barbara. "We wanted a home that was large enough for our family to come and stay with us without feeling cramped. We have enough space and enough room to really enjoy the luxury of the home itself."

Though Robert and Barbara describe themselves as conservative, they wanted a home with a modern elegance that showed through both on the exterior and interior of the home. The multi-hipped roofline, multiple transom windows and angled stairway in the Fayette seemed to capture the essence of what they were looking for.

"We were comfortable with the features that this floor plan tended to embody: the master bedroom upstairs, a family room, a formal dining room, a living room. We had all of the furniture, so we wanted to keep all of those rooms," Robert says.

Cherry cabinets, a wood floor and stained trim were detailed in the kitchen, breakfast area and an added sunroom. The same wood floor was extended along an exterior rim of the dining room with a central pad of white carpet. Painted woodwork trims the other formal areas on the main floor, while Barbara captured the elegance of the home through decorating in a style compatible with her work as a floral designer.

Robert and Barbara believe they'll build again someday, but not for a long time. "We won't get tired of this house and want to sell it while we're still working. We will have the opposite problem - getting tired enough of it so that we'll be able to part with it, when the time comes."

B. Attleboro

#48A-5083 S *Price Code A27*

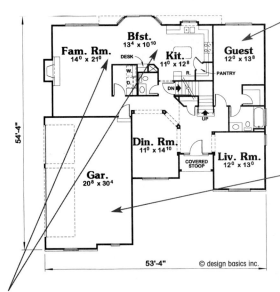

© design basics inc.

A guest suite replaced one of the formal rooms in this design offering a place for a live-in college student or nanny.

A side-load garage creates a tighter front elevation and offers an additional choice for homeowner.

The openness between this family room and kitchen is pronounced with the subtraction of walls and steps.

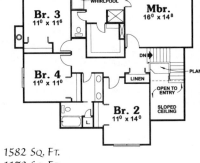

Main: 1582 Sq. Ft.
Second: 1170 Sq. Ft.

Total: 2752 Sq. Ft.

NOTE: 9 ft. main level walls

C. Stone Creek

(#48A- 8038 S) *Price Code* A24

Side by side vanities in the master suite allow the addition of an eye-appealing set of double doors.

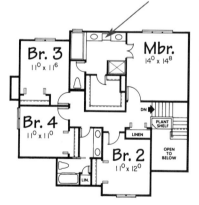

Br. 3
11⁰ x 11⁶

Mbr.
14⁰ x 14⁸

Br. 4
11⁰ x 11⁰

PLANT SHELF

LINEN

OPEN TO BELOW

Br. 2
11⁰ x 12⁰

DN

LIN.

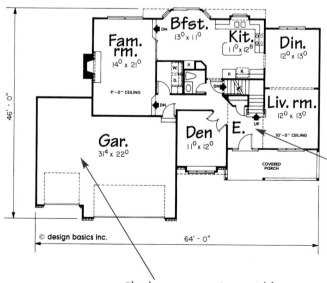

Fam. rm.
14⁰ x 21⁰
9'-0" CEILING

Bfst.
13⁰ x 11⁰

Kit.
11⁰ x 12⁸

Din.
12⁰ x 13⁰

DN

W. D.

P.

P. R.

DN

Liv. rm.
12⁰ x 13⁰

Gar.
31⁴ x 22⁰

Den
11⁰ x 12⁰

E.

UP

10'-0" CEILING

COVERED PORCH

46' - 0"

64' - 0"

© design basics inc.

The stairway is more functional in this design, yet still provides a plant shelf as a visual aid.

Main: 1379 SQ. FT.
Second: 1119 SQ. FT.

Total: 2498 SQ. FT.

The three-car garage is essential for a teenager's car or as a designated work area.

Quincy

#48A-24004 S *Price Code* A22

Bardel

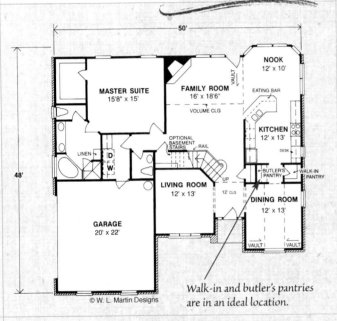

NOOK 12' x 10'

MASTER SUITE 15'8" x 15'

FAMILY ROOM 16' x 18'6"

VOLUME CLG

EATING BAR

KITCHEN 12' x 13'

DESK

OPTIONAL BASEMENT STAIRS   RAIL

LINEN

D W

50'

48'

LIVING ROOM 12' x 13'

UP

12' CLG

BUTLER'S PANTRY

WALK-IN PANTRY

DINING ROOM 12' x 13'

GARAGE 20' x 22'

VAULT   VAULT

© W. L. Martin Designs

Walk-in and butler's pantries are in an ideal location.

Guests or possibly a live-in relative will enjoy the privacy of this main-floor bedroom.

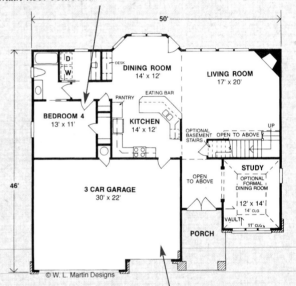

D W

DESK

DINING ROOM 14' x 12'

LIVING ROOM 17' x 20'

PANTRY

EATING BAR

BEDROOM 4 13' x 11'

50'

46'

KITCHEN 14' x 12'

OPTIONAL BASEMENT STAIRS

OPEN TO ABOVE

UP

3 CAR GARAGE 30' x 22'

OPEN TO ABOVE

STUDY OPTIONAL FORMAL DINING ROOM 12' x 14' 14' CLG

VAULT   11' CLG

PORCH

© W. L. Martin Designs

The three-car garage is minimized through the clever design of a front gable and tall entry.

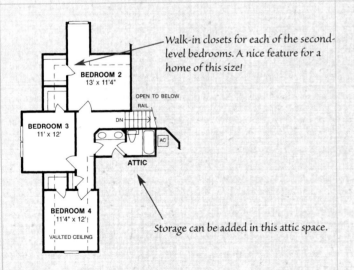

Walk-in closets for each of the second-level bedrooms. A nice feature for a home of this size!

BEDROOM 2 13' x 11'4"

OPEN TO BELOW

RAIL

BEDROOM 3 11' x 12'

DN

AC

ATTIC

BEDROOM 4 11'4" x 12'

VAULTED CEILING

Storage can be added in this attic space.

BEDROOM 2 13' x 12'

AC

MASTER SUITE 13' x 17'

OPEN TO BELOW

DN

PLAY ROOM 13' x 15'

OPTIONAL **BEDROOM 5**

OPEN TO BELOW

ATTIC   AC

BEDROOM 3 11' x 14'

Children will enjoy this designated space for play.

Main: 1568 Sq. Ft.
Second: 680 Sq. Ft.

Total: 2248 Sq. Ft.

Slab Foundation Plans Included.

Main: 1323 Sq. Ft.
Second: 1174 Sq. Ft.

Total: 2497 Sq. Ft.

Slab Foundation Plans Included.

IMPRESSIONS– *Homes designed with the look you wa*

Belle Mede

#48A-9121 S *Price Code* B33

A walk-in pantry and island counter in the kitchen are large enough to be a cook's dream!

The family room was meant for everyday enjoyment with built-in locations for TV and electronic equipment.

This home was meant to take advantage of the view to the back whether on the first or second level of the home.

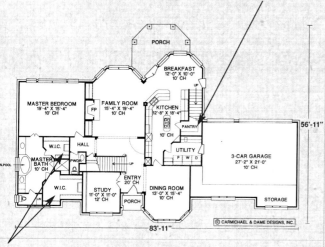

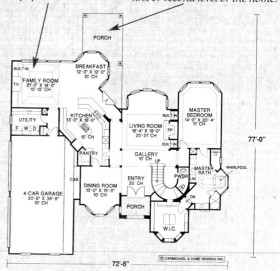

...on't miss the fact that his and her walk-in ...osets in the master suite feature built-in ...elves for clothing storage.

A large game room on the second level has a connecting sun deck and is near all second-level bedrooms.

A mid-level study includes amazing built-in bookshelves that surround the space, with three tall windows to the front.

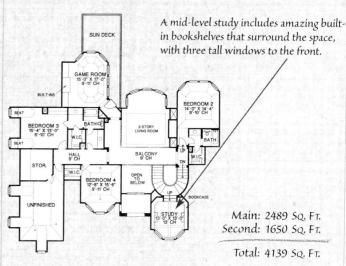

Main: 2117 Sq. Ft.
Second: 1206 Sq. Ft.

Total: 3323 Sq. Ft.

Slab and Basement Foundation Plans Included.

Main: 2489 Sq. Ft.
Second: 1650 Sq. Ft.

Total: 4139 Sq. Ft.

Optional Basement access Makes Overall Depth 81'-0"
Slab and Basement Foundation Plans Included.

DESIGN TRIO #7

A. THE QUIMBY
B. THE CHANDLER HILLS
C. THE MORENCI

ONE CONCEPT...

This floor plan features a fully-functioning main level, with all of the activity in one area, with still enough extra room for visitors. The social area of the home, the great room, is just off the entry where guests can immediately feel welcome. This is an efficient floor plan, but the thing that buyers are going to like about it, is the fact that the eating area off the kitchen has a bit more room so that it can seat a larger group and function either formally or informally. This design also provides a place to get away to, whether in the form of a porch or second living space.

3 LOOKS...

A. The exterior styling of the Quimby (at right) brings this efficient home to life. Its bold, arched entry is responsible for this, along with a symmetrically hipped roofline.

B. A simplified version, the Chandler Hills (pg. 31) offers a clean roofline, an airy front porch and the subtle touches of shutters and brick trim to draw the eye.

C. The Morenci (pg. 32) is a marriage of the other two and offers nostalgic elements to give it a sense of timelessness - thick columns above brick pedestals and batten-board shutters.

A. Quimby

#48A-3010 S   *Price Code* A14

1422 Finished Sq. Ft.

The atmosphere in the dining room is captivated by a view or a side porch and built-in bookshelves and symmetrical arches

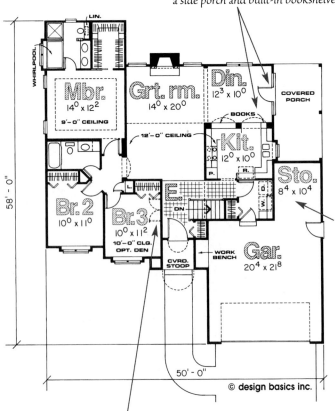

Extra space in the garage is ideal for storage, work or hobby.

Those with the need for a home office can easily add double doors to bedroom 3.

© design basics inc.

IMPRESSIONS- Homes designed with the look you wa

B. Chandler Hills

#48A-8089 S *Price Code* A14

The master suite is nicely secluded at the rear of the home, yet is still within proximity of two secondary bedrooms, for providing the attention that children need.

This snack bar will be useful in the kitchen for buffets and quick meals on the go.

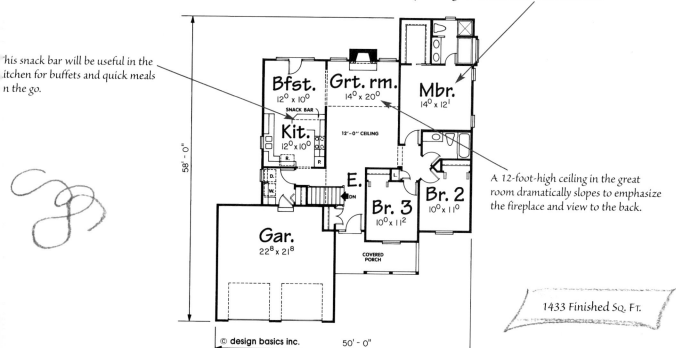

A 12-foot-high ceiling in the great room dramatically slopes to emphasize the fireplace and view to the back.

1433 Finished Sq. Ft.

© design basics inc.

C. Morenci

#48A-4953 S   *Price Code* A18

1853 Finished Sq. Ft.

NOTE: *9 ft. main level walls*

The option of an in-law suite or study gives this home added dimension.

An expanded laundry room includes a soaking sink and built-in storage shelves.

The open integration of the kitchen, dining room and great room allows greater interaction among guests and family.

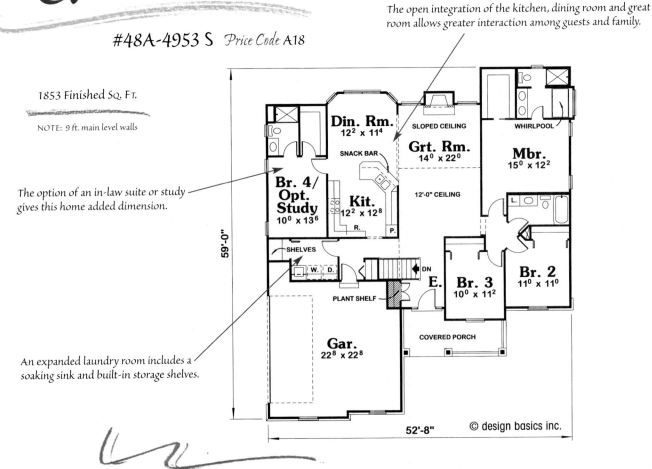

IMPRESSIONS– *Homes designed with the look you wa*

ONE CONCEPT...

This is a classic two-story home. You have good square footage, but there's not a lot of wasted space. The storage in the garage is a key element in this design. It is such a useful area for homeowners and it is not often that designs can spare such a nice area as this. You have a formal setting flush with the entry as you walk in. These areas are not large, but they serve the purpose if homeowners need to entertain. The real function of this home is for family living.

3 LOOKS...

A. All three of these elevations offer slightly different interpretations of informality. The Paisley (at left) is definitely the most polished of the three with the windows creating a charm that's pleasing to look at.

B. The Willow Grove (pg. 34) has a rustic quality to it and would look wonderful completed in a natural cedar or pine exterior. The front porch plays a prominent role on this home, spanning the entire front.

C. The Kellerton (pg. 35) looks as if it's a farmhouse from long ago with its thick rounded porch columns and full brick facade on the garage. A central gable on the second level really draws the eye to the entry as a focal point.

A. Paisley

Main: 1093 Sq. Ft.
Second: 1038 Sq. Ft.

Total: 2131 Sq. Ft.

#48A-2618 S   *Price Code A21*

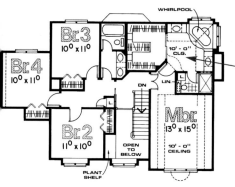

The master bath has many conveniences, including his and her compartments in a walk-in closet, separate vanities and a 10-foot-high ceiling.

A set of French doors allows both integration and separation of the two living areas.

Built-in shelves are nice features in the garage and dining room.

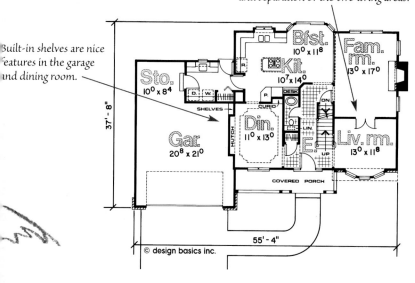

© design basics inc.

B. Willow Grove

#48A-8061 S *Price Code A21*

The family room and parlor are open to each other, allowing a smooth transition for guests.

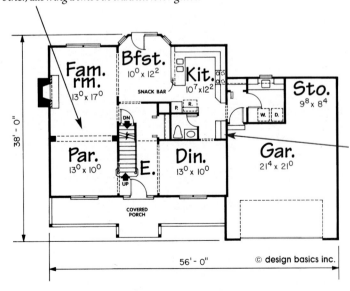

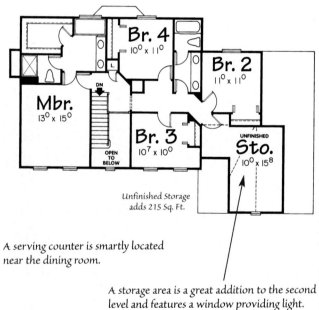

Unfinished Storage
adds 215 Sq. Ft.

A serving counter is smartly located near the dining room.

A storage area is a great addition to the second level and features a window providing light.

Main: 1086 Sq. Ft.
Second: 1033 Sq. Ft.

Total: 2119 Sq. Ft.

© design basics inc.

C. Kellerton

#48A-5499 S *Price Code* A23

A pocket door hides the laundry room, which provides a soaking sink and window.

Built-in desks are great additions to bedrooms 2 and 4.

Br.3
10⁹ x 11³

Mbr.
13⁰ x 15⁰

9'-0" CEIL.

DESK

Br.2
12⁰ x 11⁴

Br.4
11⁰ x 12⁰

DESK

OPEN TO BELOW

DN

L

STORAGE

D. W.

Bfst.
10⁴ x 14⁸

Fam.Rm
13⁰ x 17⁰

R.

Kit.
10⁶ x 13⁰

P.

DN

This island counter is a great feature in the kitchen because it allows one room to both cook and prepare food.

Gar.
21⁴ x 23⁰

Din.
11⁰ x 12⁸

E.

UP

Liv.
13⁰ x 12⁰

COVERED PORCH

39'-8"

© design basics inc.

57'-4"

Main: 1168 Sq. Ft.
Second: 1165 Sq. Ft.

Total: 2333 Sq. Ft.

NOTE: 9 ft. main level walls

Bedford

#48A-2057 S *Price Code* A22

The great room needs the tall windows in the corner to flood its large space with plenty of natural light.

Bayed windows surrounding this whirpool tub, tempt one to soak in relaxation.

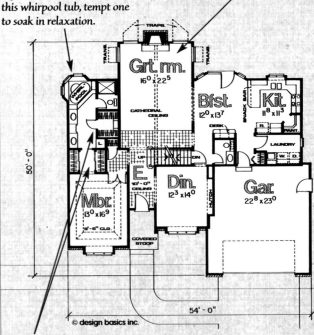

Grt. rm.
16⁰ x 22⁵
CATHEDRAL CEILING

Bfst.
12⁰ x 13⁷

Kit.
11⁸ x 11³

Mbr.
13⁰ x 16⁹
13'-6" CLG.

Din.
12³ x 14⁰

Gar.
22⁸ x 23⁰

LAUNDRY

COVERED STOOP

50' - 0"

54' - 0"

© design basics inc.

The available storage space in this home is one of its key features. Besides a second-level bonus room, there's a walk-in pantry in the kitchen and three closets in the master suite.

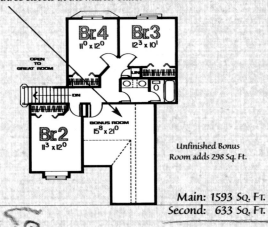

Br 4
11⁰ x 12⁰

Br 3
12³ x 10¹

OPEN TO GREAT ROOM

Br 2
11³ x 12⁰

BONUS ROOM
15⁸ x 21⁰

Unfinished Bonus Room adds 298 Sq. Ft.

Main: 1593 Sq. Ft.
Second: 633 Sq. Ft.

Total: 2226 Sq. Ft.

Kempton Court

#48A-9169 S *Price Code* B30

Diagonal halls give interest to interior spaces and channel traffic throughout the home.

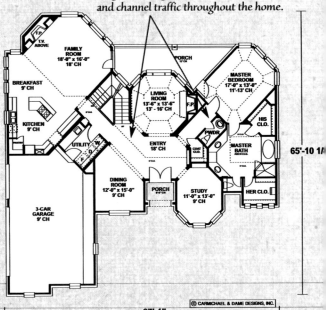

FAMILY ROOM
18'-0" x 16'-6"
18' CH

T.V. ABOVE
F.P.

PORCH
12' CH

BREAKFAST
9' CH

KITCHEN
9' CH

LIVING ROOM
13'-6" x 13'-6"
13' - 16' CH

MASTER BEDROOM
17'-8" x 13'-6"
11'-13' CH

HIS CLO.

F.P.

PWDR

MASTER BATH

UTILITY

ENTRY
18' CH

COAT CLO.

DINING ROOM
12'-0" x 15'-0"
9' CH

PORCH

STUDY
11'-8" x 13'-6"
9' CH

HER CLO.

3-CAR GARAGE
9' CH

65'-10 1/4"

67'-1"

© CARMICHAEL & DAME DESIGNS, INC.

This two-story living room will be impressive with a fireplace, bayed windows and vaulted ceiling over its two-story height.

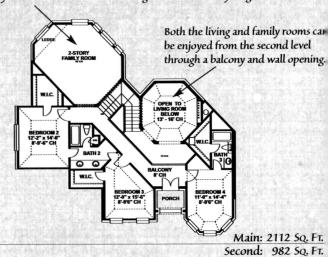

Both the living and family rooms can be enjoyed from the second level through a balcony and wall opening.

LEDGE

2-STORY FAMILY ROOM

W.I.C.

BEDROOM 2
12'-2" x 14'-4"
8'-9'-6" CH

BATH 2

OPEN TO LIVING ROOM BELOW
13' - 16' CH

W.I.C.

BATH 3

W.I.C.

BALCONY
8' CH

BEDROOM 3
12'-4" x 15'-6"
8'-9'6" CH

PORCH

BEDROOM 4
11'-6" x 14'-4"
8'-9'6" CH

Main: 2112 Sq. Ft.
Second: 982 Sq. Ft.

Slab and Basement Foundation Plans Included.

Total: 3094 Sq. Ft.

IMPRESSIONS– *Homes designed with the look you wa*

Stillwater Court

#48A-9167 S *Price Code* B29

Westminster

#48A-1815 S *Price Code* A34

An open beam ceiling exemplifies the casual atmosphere of the kitchen and family room.

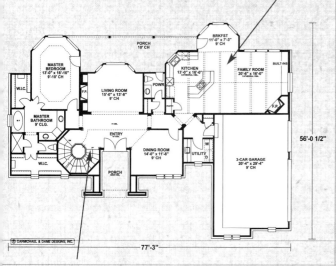

My favorite aspect of this home is its sunroom surrounded by an expansive, all-brick veranda.

This circular stair tower creates excitement not only on the front elevation, but also in the entry and living room.

A library off the master suite provides not only privacy, but also a stunning view through bayed windows.

Special care was taken to provide abundant closet space in all second-level bedrooms.

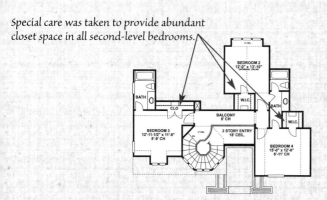

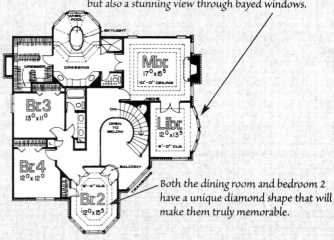

Both the dining room and bedroom 2 have a unique diamond shape that will make them truly memorable.

Main: 2044 Sq. Ft.
Second: 917 Sq. Ft.

Total: 2961 Sq. Ft.

Main: 1719 Sq. Ft.
Second: 1688 Sq. Ft.

Total: 3407 Sq. Ft.

Slab and Basement Foundation Plans Included.

HOME PLAN DESIGN SERVICE

Design Trio #9

A. The Crooked Creek
B. The Mansfield
C. The Hartwell

One Concept...

This design has notable emphasis in two areas. First, the master suite is a very important room in this design. Each of the master suites in this design trio offers a lot of options to homeowners. They are definitely get away areas. Second, there is a distinct emphasis on the formal rooms in each design. Special care was taken to create beautiful formal rooms with interesting ceiling details and window treatments. We did this for buyers who have the need to entertain and want those areas to stand out.

3 Looks...

A. Varying elevation styles are the most visible difference between each of the designs. The Crooked Creek's elevation (at right) will still appear impressive with a brick and stucco combination, but is lightened with the inclusion of a front porch.

B. The facade on the Mansfield (pg. 39), has a stately appearance and offers low maintenance, with an all-brick front.

C. On the Hartwell (pg. 40), we went back to a farmhouse appeal, providing a second entry into the home through the laundry room. Its porch is also deep enough to incorporate a swing. The absence of a formal living room inside, also fits the informal elevation style.

A. Crooked Creek

#48A-8118 S   Price Code A20

Positioning the fireplace between the kitchen and great room allows the tall windows in the great room to have enormous impact.

2079 Finished SQ. FT.

The sitting area in this master suite provides a beautiful view to the back, as well as a great place to unwind.

Extra counter space in the kitchen is in smart location to serve the dining room

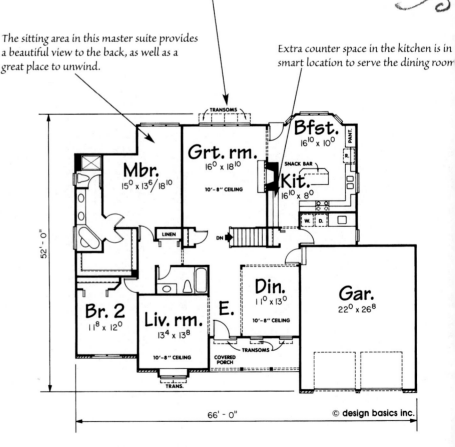

IMPRESSIONS- *Homes designed with the look you war*

B. Mansfield

#48A-1539 S *Price Code* A19

1996 Finished Sq. Ft.

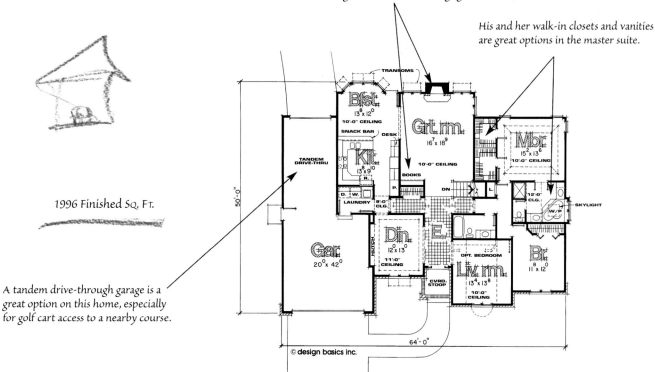

The fireplace and built-in bookcase are great accents in this large great room.

His and her walk-in closets and vanities are great options in the master suite.

A tandem drive-through garage is a great option on this home, especially for golf cart access to a nearby course.

TRANSOMS

Bfst.
13⁸ x 12
10'-0" CEILING
SNACK BAR

Grt. rm.
16⁷ x 18⁹
10'-0" CEILING

Mbr.
15² x 13⁶
10'-0" CEILING

TANDEM DRIVE-THRU

DESK

Kit.
13⁸ x 9⁰

BOOKS

12'-0" CLG.

SKYLIGHT

W/P

50'-0"

LAUNDRY
D. W.
9'-0" CLG.

P.

DN

L.

Gar.
20⁰ x 42⁰

HUTCH

Dn.
12 x 13
11'-0" CEILING

OPT. BEDROOM

Br.
11⁸ x 12

CVRD. STOOP

Liv. rm.
13⁴ x 13⁸
10'-0" CEILING

© design basics inc.

64'-0"

C. Hartwell

#48A-5498 S *Price Code A21*

This private covered porch is the ideal place for busy homeowners to unwind.

An expanded kitchen that's integrated with the great room creates options for informal entertaining.

A three-car garage is a great option for adding storage or for a teenager's car.

2188 Finished SQ. FT.

NOTE: *9 ft. main level walls*

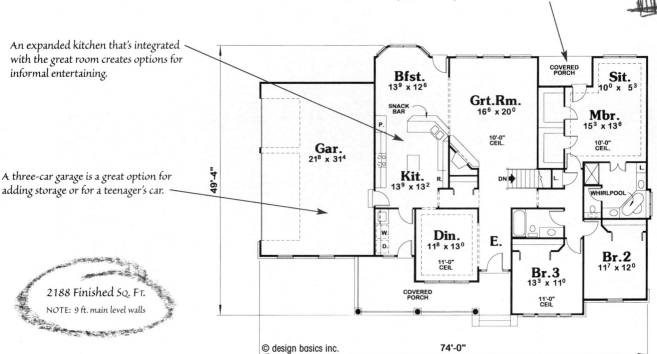

Bfst.
13⁹ x 12⁶

SNACK BAR

P.

Gar.
21⁸ x 31⁴

Grt.Rm.
16⁶ x 20⁰

10'-0" CEIL.

COVERED PORCH

Sit.
10⁰ x 5³

Mbr.
15³ x 13⁶

10'-0" CEIL.

Kit.
13⁹ x 13²

R.

DN

L.

L.

L.

WHIRLPOOL

49'-4"

W.

D.

Din.
11⁸ x 13⁰

11'-0" CEIL

E.

Br.3
13³ x 11⁰

11'-0" CEIL.

Br.2
11⁷ x 12⁰

COVERED PORCH

© design basics inc.

74'-0"

BUILT BY: Webb Development Co.

BUILT BY: Dale Yost Construction

Beaumont

48A-1388 S *Price Code* A22

The kitchen not only enjoys a see-through fireplace, but it also has view of a stunning six-sided breakfast area with bayed windows.

With built-in bookcase and view to the back, this private den will be a great place to work.

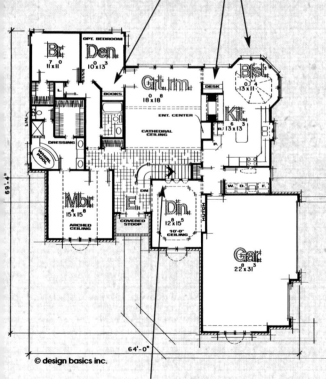

© design basics inc.

Subtle touches in the dining room make it truly elegant – a decorative ceiling, arched window and triple openings viewing past the stairway.

2254 Finished Sq. Ft.

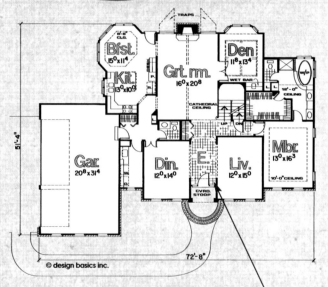

© design basics inc.

Large living and dining rooms are showpieces in the entry and allow plenty of room for guests to circulate.

A second-floor balcony allows all to admire the great room's trapezoid windows and cathedral ceiling.

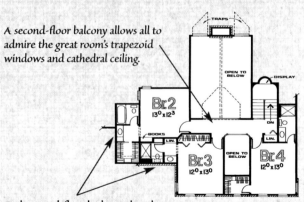

Each second-floor bedroom has the convenience of a separate bath.

Main: 2063 Sq. Ft.
Second: 894 Sq. Ft.

Total: 2957 Sq. Ft.

HOME OWNER IMPRESSIONS
ON LIVING IN THE BRADBURY

After 30 years in the real estate industry, Edith has seen a lot of homes. So when it came time for her to retire, it would've seemed that the home she'd choose would be reflected in the many things she'd seen and pointed out to client after client over the years.

As it turns out, the home Edith elected to build tells less about what she's seen and admired in the industry and more about her own interests and needs.

"To me, it was about simplifying my life. I'd had the big house, raised my children, had the fancy furnishings. I was done with that. I wanted a home for me," Edith says.

Three years ago, still going strong at age 56, Edith's children - three sons and a daughter - were pressuring her to think about retiring soon. She mentioned this fact to a long-time friend in the industry, a builder with whom she'd worked for over 20 years.

After looking at home plans off and on for nearly a year with Edith, her builder friend received a new Design Basics plan book in the mail. He convinced Edith to come over to look through it that day. One of the homes he had flagged for her was the Bradbury.

"It was the first plan that really caught my eye right away. It seemed as though all the other plans I'd looked at either had something I didn't want, or had extra space that I didn't need.

continued on page 44

The master bedroom is provided the best of both worlds - close proximity to two other bedrooms, yet optimum seclusion.

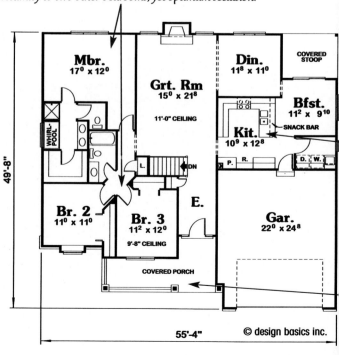

IMPRESSIONS- *Homes designed with the look you wa*

A. *Bradbury*

#48A-4948 S *Price Code* A17

The option of a snack bar creates more
room to serve meals and guests informally.

1758 Finished SQ. FT.

NOTE: 9 ft. main level walls

— The addition of a porch to the front
of this home emphasizes its casual state.

ONE CONCEPT...

The central appeal of this floor plan lies in its unique kitchen core. It provides close proximity to both formal and informal eating areas and is just steps from the garage. A rear covered porch is the best element of all - just enough of a get-away to relax after cooking or enjoying an evening meal. The great room provides the expansive room for entertaining guests, whether family or friends. And all the bedrooms are neatly tucked away from the activity areas of the home, for privacy.

3 LOOKS...

A. Subtle elevation details, on the Bradbury (at left) such as window brackets, Doric columns and batten-board shutters lend antiquity to its quiet appearance.

B. A pleasing roofline carries the pared-down front elevation of the Quail Hollow (pg. 44), nicely adjoining its prominent window arrangement.

C. Stucco is an effective treatment on the Monterey (pg. 45) because of its pairing with brick and its defining moulding that draws attention to a palladian window and the entry.

Every space seemed to have a purpose in this home. It seemed to have everything I needed and nothing more - which was the way I wanted it," Edith says.

Besides her four children, Edith has three grandchildren - all of whom visit nearly every Sunday. So the Bradbury's two extra bedrooms were a must for her, as well as the large great room, where they all gather, she says, after Sunday dinner.

"It's big enough so the kids can play at one end of the room and we adults can talk at the other end. I like the fact that it's big enough for all of us to be together," she says.

Edith not only wanted a large great room, but she also wanted a smaller living area that she could use on an everyday basis. She altered the home's dining room into a sunroom with French doors that lead out onto the back porch.

"In the cooler months I spend almost everyday in the sunroom and in the warmer months I spend my time out on the porch."

And though she'd like everyone to think she's retired, to this day she still get referrals from past clients and will still occasionally show homes. As more of a hobby these days, she watches the sales and new listings, accessing them through a computer she has set up in the master suite.

Edith says she has never enjoyed any home she's lived in or shown to a client, as much as this home.

"One thing I've learned being a real estate agent, is that there are a lot of beautiful homes out there, but they aren't always right for everyone. This home is the first home I've lived in that really reflects me."

B. Quail Hollow

#48A- 8069 S *Price Code* A17

1729 Finished Sq. Ft.

Transoms above two large windows in the great room extend the view to the back.

This master bath emphasizes more functionality than luxury and compartmentalizes the stool.

The dining room and great room easily expand into one another.

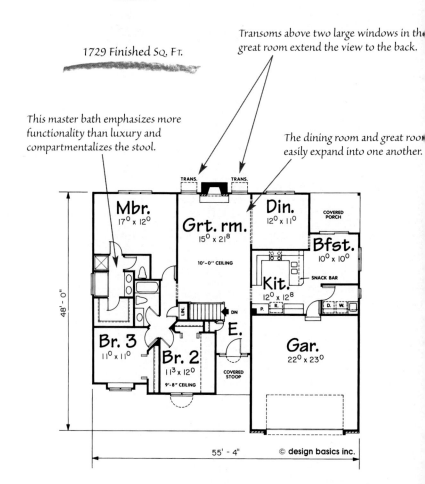

© design basics inc.

C. Monterey

#48A-2290 S *Price Code* A16

1666 Finished SQ. FT.

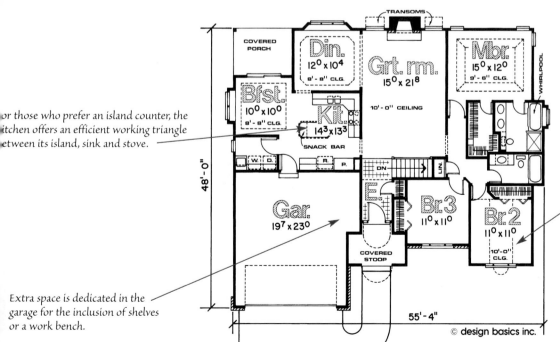

or those who prefer an island counter, the itchen offers an efficient working triangle etween its island, sink and stove.

Bedroom 2 will make the ideal guest suite with its 10-foot sloped ceiling and beautiful windows.

Extra space is dedicated in the garage for the inclusion of shelves or a work bench.

COVERED PORCH

Din. 12⁰ x 10⁴
8'-8" CLG.

Grt. rm. 15⁰ x 21⁸
10'-0" CEILING

Mbr. 15⁰ x 12⁰
9'-6" CLG.

TRANSOMS

WHIRLPOOL

Bfst. 10⁰ x 10⁰
8'-8" CLG.

Kit. 14³ x 13³
SNACK BAR

W. D.   R.   P.   DN   LIN

Gar. 19⁷ x 23⁰

Br. 3 11⁰ x 11⁰

Br. 2 11⁰ x 11⁰
10'-0" CLG.

COVERED STOOP

48'-0"

55'-4"

© design basics inc.

Roxbury

#48A-2848 S *Price Code* A21

A see-through fireplace will give an extra sense of coziness to the kitchen and breakfast area.

Tall windows at the front and back of this home allow interior rooms to be filled with light.

The bayed hearth room is a wonderful second living area with not only warmth, but also plenty of natural light.

The separation of the master suite gives this home a great deal of privac

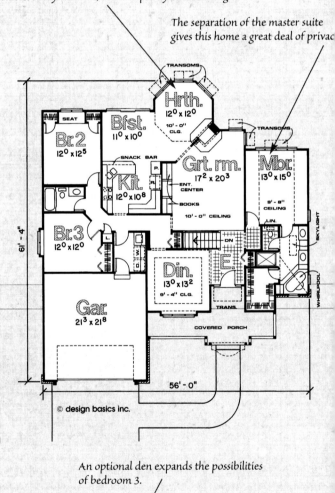

What a charming bedroom with sloped ceiling and window seat between two closets!

2148 Finished Sq. Ft.

An optional den expands the possibilities of bedroom 3.

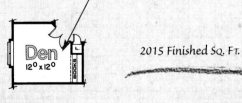

2015 Finished Sq. Ft.

IMPRESSIONS— *Homes designed with the look you wa*

#48A-3156 S *Price Code* A32

Schuyler

#48A-4134 S *Price Code* A26

Elements in the master bath were positioned for ultimate symmetry. A whirlpool tub sits across from a diamond-shaped shower, between his and her vanities.

A side porch creates a convenient mud entry when doing yard work.

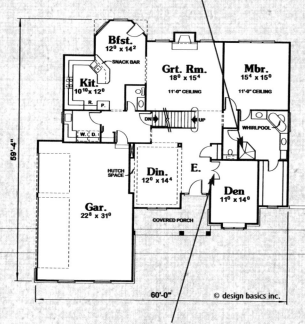

© design basics inc.

With double doors off the entry, the den would make an ideal home office.

© design basics inc.

A bonus room provides great additional space in this home that can be finished into an exercise area, bedroom suite or hobby room.

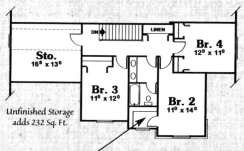

Bonus Room adds 534 Sq. Ft.

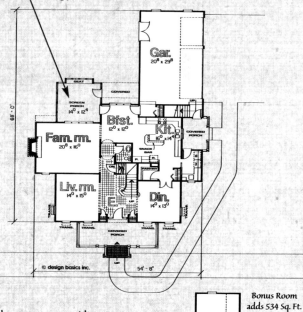

Unfinished Storage adds 232 Sq. Ft.

Bedroom 2 offers space for toy storage in its walk-in closet.

Main: 1847 Sq. Ft.
Second: 766 Sq. Ft.

Total: 2613 Sq. Ft.

NOTE: 9 ft. main level walls

Main: 1598 Sq. Ft.
Second: 1675 Sq. Ft.

Total: 3273 Sq. Ft.

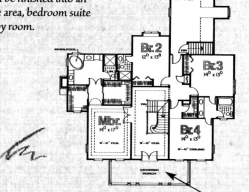

A covered porch is a great place to enjoy the outdoors without suffering its elements.

DESIGN TRIO #11

A. THE HOLDEN
B. THE COOPERS FARM
C. THE GREENSBORO

ONE CONCEPT...

This home plan offers a lot of typical options for homebuyers, but in a little bit different placement, depending on a buyer's personal preference for an elevation. First, all of these homes feature a great outdoor area to relax, located in either the front or rear of the home. This design also designates a place to formally entertain, whether a buyer wants both a formal living and dining room or just a dining room to be used in conjunction with the great room. Another nice option in this design is the inclusion of space for an office or den. Many buyers find this to be an important feature.

3 LOOKS...

A. I think the Holden (at right) seems to marry the two very different styles that follow it by offering a mostly brick elevation. The combination creates an unpretentious, yet polished effect.

B. On the comfortable, country-styled Coopers Farm, (pg. 49) we designed a large front porch, carved posts and a decorative arch detail. Brick serves as merely a detail here with the emphasis on a more relaxed styling.

C. Nearly opposite in appeal is the Greensboro (pg. 50). Here we designed the full brick front and quoin detail to make it feel grand and a bit more upscale. The symmetry in its windows also helps balance its wide elevation.

A. Holden

#48A-4998 S   Price Code A2

This large storage area in the garage will be welcome for lawn equipment and bikes.

Mbr. 13⁰ x 15⁶

Grt. Rm. 16⁰ x 20⁰

Bfst. 10⁰ x 13⁸

Kit. 11⁰ x 13⁸

Gar. 21⁰ x 21⁴

WHIRL-POOL

Br. 2 11⁰ x 12⁰

Br. 3/ Opt. Liv. Rm. 12⁰ x 11⁰

E.

Din. Rm. 12⁰ x 15⁵

Office/ Opt. Br. 4 11⁰ x 13⁵

Stor.

DN

COVERED PORCH

48'-8"

76'-8"

© design basics inc.

The second option of the living room/bedroom allows this home to grow with a family.

This secluded room will make a great office, with side door for clients, or an in-law suite, with close proximity to a full bath.

2227 Finished Sq. Ft.

NOTE: 9 ft. main level walls

IMPRESSIONS- Homes designed with the look you wa

B. Coopers Farm

#48A-8045 S *Price Code A21*

Tall ceilings throughout the living and sleeping areas add an extra sense of spaciousness.

A soaking sink and a hanging rod above, expand the uses of the laundry room.

An enjoyable master bath reveals a soaking tub and dual-sink vanity with knee space - all behind a set of French doors.

TRANSOMS

Mbr.
13⁰ x 16⁵

Grt. rm.
16⁰ x 20⁰
10'-0" CEILING

Bfst.
10⁰ x 11⁴

Kit.
8¹⁰ x 13⁸

PANT. R.

D. W.

Gar.
21⁰ x 25⁴

40' - 0"

Br. 2
11⁰ x 13⁰
9'-0" CEILING

Br. 3
12⁰ x 11⁴
10'-0" CEILING

E.

DN

Din.
12⁰ x 15⁴
10'-0" CEILING

Off.
11⁰ x 18⁰
9'-0" CEILING

COVERED   PORCH

76' - 8"

© design basics inc.

2151 Finished SQ. FT.

C. Greensboro

#48A-2326 S *Price Code* A21

Tall windows in the great room and master bed-room are good sources for views and light.

The kitchen offers great benefits, such as an island counter and corner walk-in pantry.

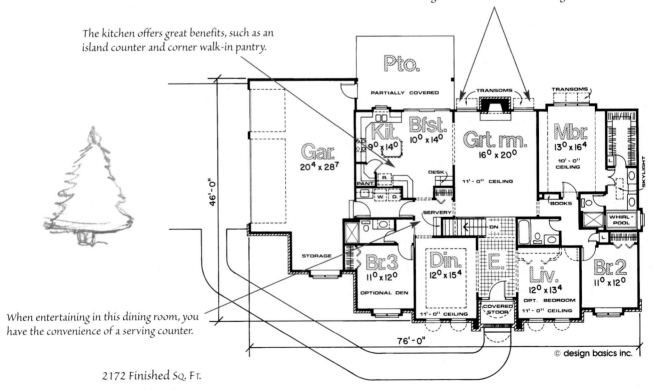

When entertaining in this dining room, you have the convenience of a serving counter.

2172 Finished Sq. Ft.

A. Hannifan Lane

#48A-8065 S *Price Code A20*

ONE CONCEPT...

We designed this floor plan to be very versatile and you will see that from the variety of options we offer on the following three examples. This home was meant for a family and so there are a couple of key areas where we did not compromise, believing they were very important to a family. First, this design has a nice-sized laundry room. It is located right off the garage and includes a soaking sink. Its location cuts down on the noise level within a home and its size is appropriate to family needs. The kitchen features a snack bar, which in today's day and age can be important for a family. With kids involved in many activities, always coming and going, its just easier for them to sit down at the snack bar while a parent serves them a quick meal than to get together at the dinner table.

3 LOOKS...

A. *The Hannifan Lane (at left) has a lot of presence, not only because of its three-car garage, but also because of its use of brick in a prominent way and the absence of porch railings which give you a feeling for its size and depth.*

B. *The Paterson (pg. 52) is another great design with a long roofline that's broken up by a second level gable. The porch and side window combine with the second-level window to give it appropriate balance.*

C. *Three dormers on the Castine (pg. 53) were designed to give the elevation eye-catching appeal and also take some of the emphasis off the garage. The three-car garage is tucked under the roofline, which makes it less noticeable and the elevation cleaner.*

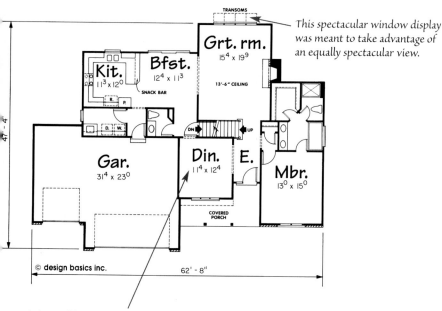

This spectacular window display was meant to take advantage of an equally spectacular view.

© design basics inc.

62' - 8"

Holidays will be extra-special because of the inclusion of a dining room in this design.

The size and shape of this bonus room makes it a great candidate for a living space.

Main: 1411 Sq. Ft.
Second: 618 Sq. Ft.

Total: 2029 Sq. Ft.

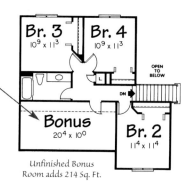

Unfinished Bonus Room adds 214 Sq. Ft.

B. Paterson

#48A-1380 S *Price Code* A19

Main: 1421 SQ. FT.
Second: 578 SQ. FT.

Total: 1999 SQ. FT.

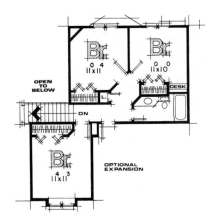

What a great atmosphere the see-through fireplace will create in the breakfast area!

A corner walk-in pantry is an effic[...] feature in this compact kitchen.

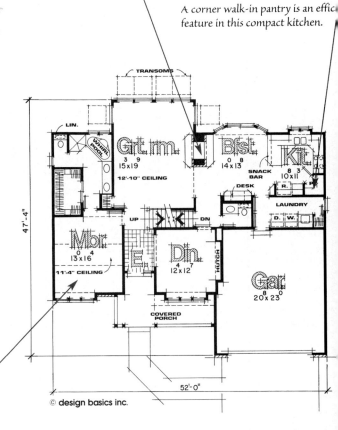

The more than 11-foot-high ceiling in this master suite will call attention to everything below.

© design basics inc.

IMPRESSIONS- *Homes designed with the look you w[...]*

C. Castine

#48A-5132 S *Price Code* A25

A live-in relative or older child will appreciate the privacy of this optional bedroom.

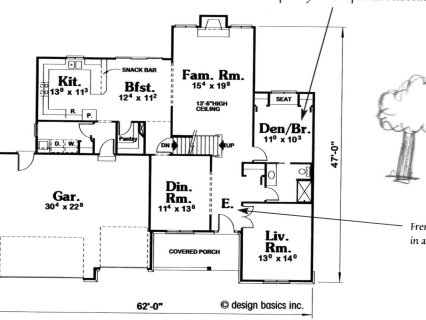

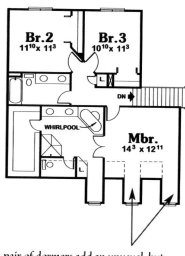

A pair of dormers add an unusual, but pleasing dimension to the master bedroom.

French doors enclose this living room, which is in an ideal location to entertain or greet guests.

Main: 1544 SQ. FT.
Second: 962 SQ. FT.

Total: 2506 SQ. FT.

NOTE: 9 ft. main level walls

BUILT BY: Southfork Homes

Ashworth

#48A-3103 S *Price Code* A17

Stratman

#48A-3588 S *Price Code* A21

BUILT BY: Ron Mahoney Builder

While double doors keep the kitchen out of view in the entry, what is visible is a staircase with pleasant style.

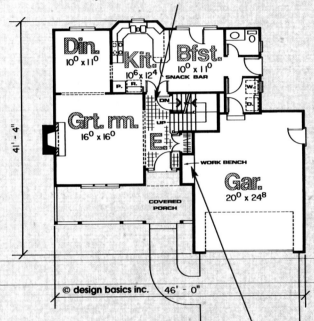

A pair of living areas plus a built-in wet bar make entertaining easy.

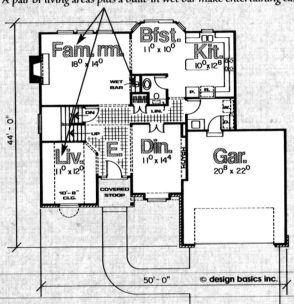

A built-in workbench in the garage will be welcome for projects of all kinds.

Each additional bedroom is given unique features, such as window seats or an arched window with sloped ceiling.

This walk-in closet can easily be enlarged, by tapping into unfinished storage space.

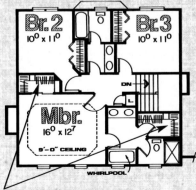

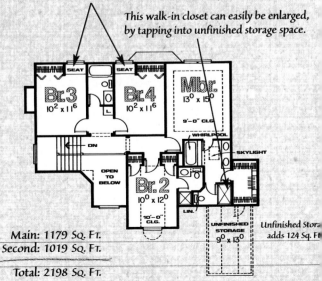

For a home of this efficiency, his and her walk-in closets are a great design element in the master suite.

Main: 904 Sq. Ft.
Second: 796 Sq. Ft.

Total: 1700 Sq. Ft.

Main: 1179 Sq. Ft.
Second: 1019 Sq. Ft.

Total: 2198 Sq. Ft.

Unfinished Stora
adds 124 Sq. Ft

54

IMPRESSIONS- Homes designed with the look you wo

BUILT BY: Byers Construction

Marshall

48A-2208 S *Price Code* A23

The addition of a hearth room allows the great room to take on a more formal function, if necessary.

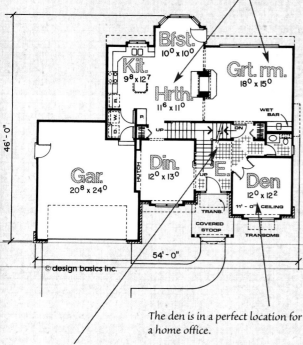

© design basics inc.

The den is in a perfect location for a home office.

Because of the many living spaces in this home, the T-shaped staircase is important to efficiently access the second level.

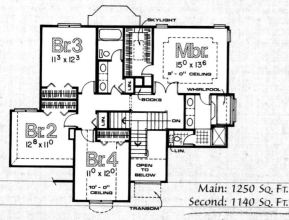

Main: 1250 SQ. FT.
Second: 1140 SQ. FT.

Total: 2390 SQ. FT.

Kingsbury

BUILT BY: Quail Valley Homes

Built-in bookcases are nice accents in the hearth room and great room.

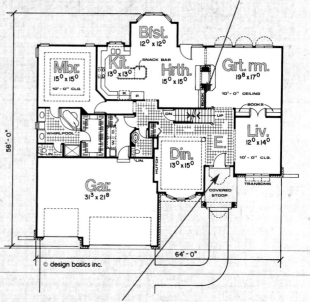

© design basics inc.

This elevation has a great sense of style with a copper-clad eave and gently sweeping arch over the entry.

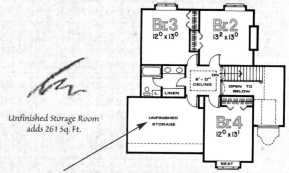

Unfinished Storage Room adds 261 Sq. Ft.

This storage area has the potential to be finished into an exercise area or playroom.

Main: 2073 SQ. FT.
Second: 741 SQ. FT.

Total: 2814 SQ. FT.

HOME PLAN DESIGN SERVICE

Design Trio #13

A. The Brook Valley
B. The Bermier
C. The Bowden

One Concept...

This floor plan has everything you would expect for a typical 1 1/2-story home. It features a dining room just inside the entry, which serves as a focal point. And straight ahead, the great room draws you to it with a fireplace between a pair of windows. The master suite is secluded on the main floor, away from the activity. But one thing you would not expect in a typical home is the large storage area located on the second floor. This really helps set this design apart and make it attractive to homebuyers.

3 Looks...

A. The Brook Valley (at right) is very straightforward with front-to-back gables and the second level window stacked over the dining room. This elevation not only breaks up the roof a bit, but it also creates emphasis on its front porch, which is definitely more noticeable on this elevation.

B. The Bermier (pg. 57) has a lot of roof to accent its second level gable. The roof runs all the way down to the porch, so you really appreciate the interesting lines the roof creates on the elevation.

C. The Bowden (pg. 58) holds steadfast in traditional roots. Everything about this elevation seems in proportion and balanced. And with its side-load garage, the facade is much more closely aligned, giving it its "cottage" appeal.

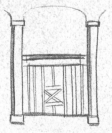

A. Brook Valley

#48A-8084 S   *Price Code A18*

A two-story great room is naturally impressive and dramatic.

Corner windows in the kitchen offer a view while preparing or cleaning up after meals.

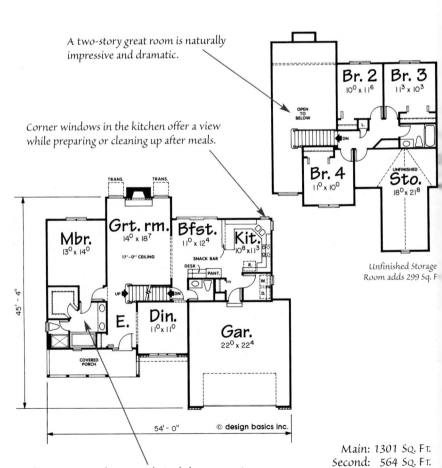

Unfinished Storage Room adds 299 Sq. Ft.

This master suite has every desired element - a sizeable walk-in closet, dual-sink vanity, soaking tub and compartmented shower.

Main: 1301 Sq. Ft.
Second: 564 Sq. Ft.

Total: 1865 Sq. Ft.

IMPRESSIONS- Homes designed with the look you w...

B. Bermier

#48A-2236 S *Price Code* A18

These corner windows make a spectacular view at this end of the great room.

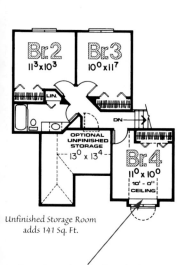

Br. 2
11³x10³

Br. 3
10⁰x11⁷

LIN.

DN

OPTIONAL
UNFINISHED
STORAGE
13⁰ x 13⁴

Br. 4
11⁰ x 10⁰
10'-0"
CEILING

Unfinished Storage Room
adds 141 Sq. Ft.

A boxed window with arch along with a sloped ceiling define this bedroom.

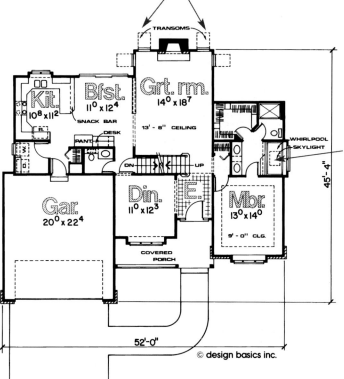

TRANSOMS

Kit.
10⁸x11²

Bfst.
11⁰ x 12⁴

Grt. rm.
14⁰ x 18⁷

13'-8" CEILING

SNACK BAR

DESK

PANT.

WHIRLPOOL
SKYLIGHT

DN   UP

Gar.
20⁰ x 22⁴

Din.
11⁰ x 12³

E.

Mbr.
13⁰ x 14⁰

9'-0" CLG.

COVERED
PORCH

45'-4"

52'-0"

© design basics inc.

I imagine nothing would be more wonderful than relaxing in this whirlpool tub with the warm glow of a skylight above.

Main: 1297 Sq. Ft.
Second: 558 Sq. Ft.

Total: 1855 Sq. Ft.

design basics inc.
HOME PLAN DESIGN SERVICE

C. Bowden

#48A-5148 S *Price Code A23*

This large kitchen with curved snack bar was meant for guests to mingle around a buffet.

A set of double doors on this master suite suggest an element of privacy.

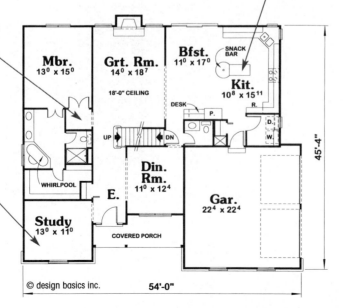

Mbr. 13⁰ x 15⁰

Grt. Rm. 14⁰ x 18⁷
18'-0" CEILING

Bfst. 11⁰ x 17⁰

SNACK BAR

Kit. 10⁸ x 15¹¹

DESK

P.

R.

UP

DN

D.

W.

WHIRLPOOL

E.

Din. Rm. 11⁰ x 12⁴

Gar. 22⁴ x 22⁴

45'-4"

This study is positioned to be versatile whether needed as a place to entertain or keep the family computer.

Study 13⁰ x 11⁰

COVERED PORCH

© design basics inc.

54'-0"

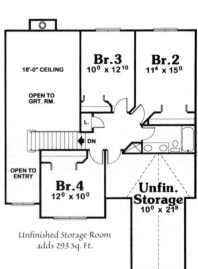

18'-0" CEILING

OPEN TO GRT. RM.

Br.3 10⁰ x 12¹⁰

Br.2 11⁴ x 15⁰

L.

DN

OPEN TO ENTRY

Br.4 12⁰ x 10⁰

Unfin. Storage 10⁰ x 21⁸

Unfinished Storage Room adds 293 Sq. Ft.

Main: 1665 Sq. Ft.
Second: 674 Sq. Ft.

Total: 2339 Sq. Ft.

NOTE: 9 ft. main level walls

IMPRESSIONS- *Homes designed with the look you wa*

#48A-1805 S *Price Code* A25

Marlow

48A-4144 S *Price Code* A30

...rtainly one of the most enjoyable aspects of this home will be ...e kitchen, equipped with a walk-in pantry, double oven, island ...oktop and large snack bar.

The kitchen, breakfast area and hearth room offer a spacious place to relax at the end of the day.

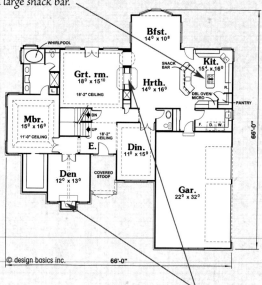

© design basics inc.

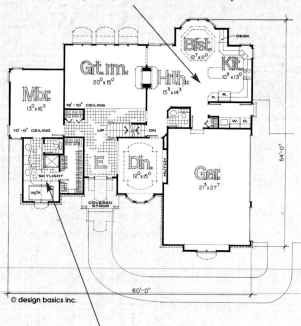

© design basics inc.

A fireplace is a relaxing component to the den, great room and hearth room.

The master bath has many comforts - a skylit vanity, wide whirlpool tub and expansive walk-in closet.

On the second level, three large bedrooms are provided a compartmented bath.

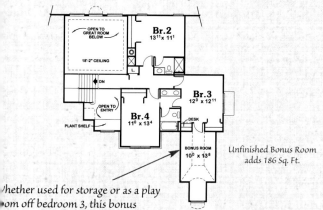

Unfinished Bonus Room adds 186 Sq. Ft.

...hether used for storage or as a play ...om off bedroom 3, this bonus ...om will be a welcome feature.

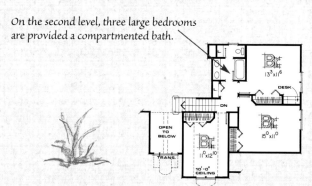

Main: 2215 SQ. FT.
Second: 825 SQ. FT.

Total: 3040 SQ. FT.

Main: 1765 SQ. FT.
Second: 743 SQ. FT.

Total: 2508 SQ. FT.

NOTE: 9 ft. main level walls

HOME OWNER IMPRESSIONS

ON LIVING IN THE TECOMA

When James and Sylvia decided to relocate to the East Coast from their Midwest home of 15 years, they thought they would never again find a place that would feel like home. Just two years ago, James and Sylvia paid their first visit to a private New England college where James had accepted a position as vice president. That afternoon, the couple decided to take a leisurely drive through town to get to know the area, for which they immediately developed a strong liking. Exploring new housing developments, they met Alan, a local builder and developer.

"Both of the homes that he was working on were sold, but he did offer to show us his plans for a home on another lot close by. We met with him a few days later and found it met our needs quite well. We decided to go ahead and build it," Sylvia says.

The home was Design Basics' Tecoma. "Everything about it seemed right for us," Sylvia says. "It was within our budget. It was a step up from our previous home. It was relatively close to the university. We just didn't see any reason to look at any other plans."

One of Sylvia's favorite aspects of the design is the master bath. Originally, Sylvia says, she was convinced that she did not want a whirlpool tub because she thought she would never use it. However, Alan, felt they would regret it if they did not put one in. "After going back and fourth for several days, I finally gave in and we compromised on a garden tub. And I have to admit, I use it at least three times a week. And even if I didn't use it, it really

Volume ceilings in the kitchen and breakfast area will emphasiz the open feel of the home.

Grt. Rm. 15⁰ x 18⁷
10'-0"HIGH CEILING

Bfst. 11⁰ x 12³
SNACK BAR
10'-0"HIGH CEILING

Kit. 10⁸ x 11³
DESK
P.
R.
D.
W.

WHIRL-POOL
UP
DN

Mbr. 13⁰ x 16⁰
E.
PORCH
Din. Rm. 11⁰ x 12⁴
Gar. 22⁰ x 23⁴

46'-4"
55'-0"

© design basics inc.

continued on page 62

IMPRESSIONS- Homes designed with the look you wa

DESIGNERS'INK

A. Tecoma

#48A-5160 S *Price Code* A17

This side-load garage is hidden by an attractive facade and permits direct access into the home.

A nearly floor-to-ceiling window creates visual excitement in Bedroom 3.

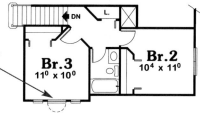

DN L.

Br.3
11^0 x 10^0

Br.2
10^4 x 11^0

Main: 1363 Sq. Ft.
Second: 399 Sq. Ft.

Total: 1762 Sq. Ft.

NOTE: 9 ft. main level walls

DESIGN TRIO #14

A. THE TECOMA
B. THE SUN VALLEY
C. THE TYNDALE

ONE CONCEPT...

The connected, open line between the kitchen, breakfast area and great room creates the continuity of this design. Whether entertaining or interacting on a daily basis with one's family, this convenient layout eases room-to-room traffic. The breakfast area naturally extends into an L-shaped cove - a perfect place to add a deck or patio. The dining room allows the ability to formally entertain and the separate master suite results in the ideal privacy for parents.

3 LOOKS...

A. The Tecoma's (at left) elevation looks a bit more distinguished because of its subtle detailing: the use of double-hung windows, dentil moulding beneath a palladian-arch window, and square columns to frame the entry and dining room window.

B. The simplified elevation of the Sun Valley (pg. 62) is nevertheless appealing because of its stacked roofline and prominent windows.

C. Stone gives the Tyndale's (pg. 63) front elevation just the casual touch it needs. An equally exciting roofline helps further define the home.

makes the bath something special."

James and Sylvia agree the kitchen, great room and breakfast area is one of the most utilized areas of the home. "The ten foot ceilings from the great room to the kitchen feel open and comfortable. Every one of our friends and family who've come to visit us think we've moved into this huge home. But when we tell them the square footage, they can't believe it. And to us it really feels large too," Sylvia says.

Though a dining room isn't a big consideration for many homebuyers these days, Sylvia and James were glad the Tecoma incorporated one. Sylvia, the oldest in her family, inherited a dining room set made by her great-grandfather, a furniture maker who emigrated from Italy. The set contains a tea service cart, dining room table, hutch and six chairs.

"The dining room set is near and dear to our family so it's really nice to have a place to display it in our home. It also seems to fit the traditional nature of the home," Sylvia says.

Though their dining room is only used on special occasions, it has come to serve a secondary purpose in their home, according to James. As a college president, they have to frequently entertain, and the dining room set has become a wonderful conversation piece. "Now, many people have heard about the dining room set even before they've visited our home," James says.

Though it's been just over one year since they've lived in the Tecoma, both Sylvia and James agree they've once again found a place they can call home.

B. Sun Valley

#48A- 8095 S *Price Code* A16

The tall transom windows in the great room not only allow an extended view to the back, they also bring in needed light to fill the expanse of the room.

A large snack bar in the kitchen, allows one to enjoy a meal or snack while conversing with those in the kitchen.

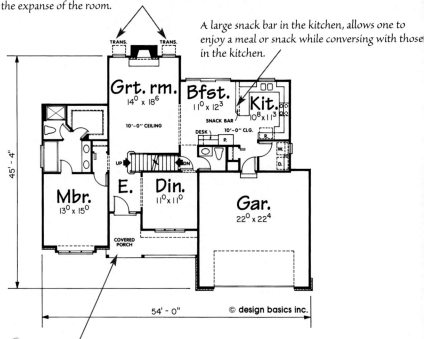

On this home, the front porch is the ideal element to draw outsiders into the entry.

Main: 1298 SQ. FT.
Second: 396 SQ. FT.

Total: 1694 SQ. FT.

IMPRESSIONS- *Homes designed with the look you wa*

C. Tyndale

#48A-2245 S *Price Code* **A16**

An 11-foot-high ceiling in the master bath is given further impact with a large skylight above the whirlpool tub.

A half wall brings some definition to the breakfast area, yet continues the open connection with the great room.

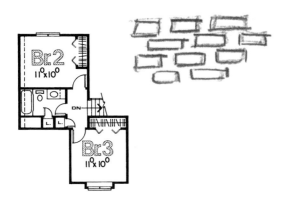

Br. 2
11⁰x10⁰

DN

Br. 3
11⁰x10⁰

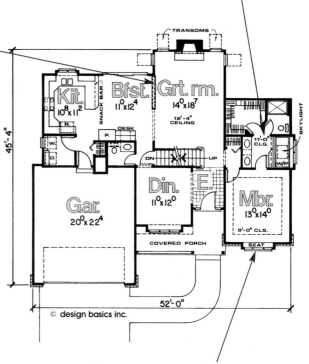

TRANSOMS

Kit.
10⁰x11²

Bfst.
11⁰x12⁴

Grt. rm.
14⁰x18⁷

12'-4" CEILING

SNACK BAR

DESK

11'-0" CLG.

SKYLIGHT

45'-4"

Gar.
20⁰x22⁴

Din.
11⁰x12⁰

Mbr.
13⁰x14⁰

9'-0" CLG.

W/P

SEAT

COVERED PORCH

52'-0"

© design basics inc.

Main: 1297 Sq. Ft.
Second: 388 Sq. Ft.

Total: 1685 Sq. Ft.

Another quaint aspect to the master suite is its built-in window seat - a great spot for reading.

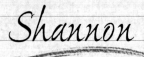

Shannon

#48A-2218 S *Price Code* A19

Rowena

#48A-5178 S *Price Code* A26

Most wouldn't notice this rear porch, which, I suppose, is the point of its seclusion.

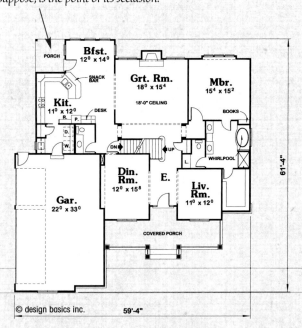

Guests and family can easily circulate in this expansive great room.

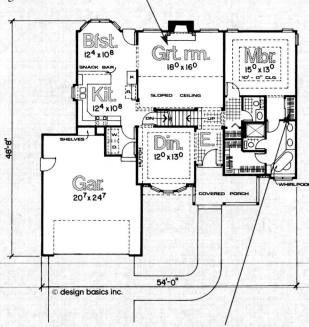

A computer desk or pair of chairs would fit nicely in an alcove located in bedroom 3.

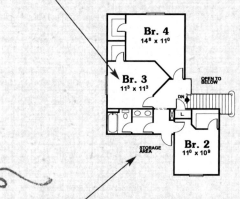

A second closet in the master suite offers a great spot for seasonal clothing storage.

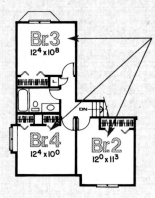

The large second-level bedrooms will be especially appreciated in this family home.

The second level can be expanded by developing this unfinished storage area.

Main: 1870 Sq. Ft.
Second: 767 Sq. Ft.

Total: 2637 Sq. Ft.

Main: 1348 Sq. Ft.
Second: 603 Sq. Ft.

Total: 1951 Sq. Ft.

NOTE: 9 ft. main level walls

IMPRESSIONS– *Homes designed with the look you wa.*

Chilton

#48A-3377 S *Price Code* A25

By sharing a see-thru fireplace, both the family and living rooms have great visual appeal at each end.

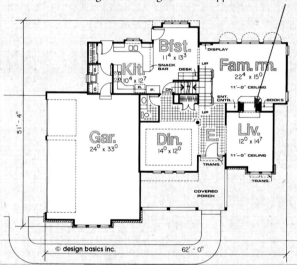

This wet bar can be accessed for formal serving to the dining room, as well as casual entertaining throughout the home.

A private den with built-in bookshelves provides privacy for studying or reading.

The walk-in closet in the master suite has the ability to expand into a large storage area.

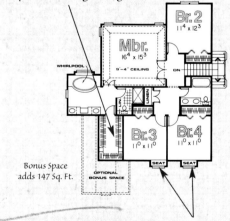

Bonus Space adds 147 Sq. Ft.

Children and adults alike will enjoy the window seats in bedrooms 3 and 4.

Main: 1406 Sq. Ft.
Second: 1137 Sq. Ft.

Total: 2543 Sq. Ft.

The amount of space in the laundry room is exceptional. It includes freezer space, a built-in ironing board and a large counter area for folding clothes or completing household projects.

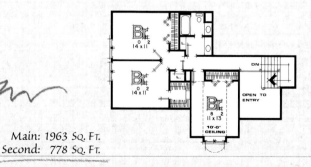

Main: 1963 Sq. Ft.
Second: 778 Sq. Ft.

Total: 2741 Sq. Ft.

DESIGN TRIO #15

A. THE SHAWNEE
B. THE McCLELLAN
C. THE INDIAN SPRINGS

ONE CONCEPT...

There are still many homebuyers who desire a dining room in addition to an informal breakfast area. This design will appeal to these buyers because it includes a dining room yet maintains a very controlled square footage range. The dining room also offers a nice formal setting that is immediately within view when you walk in. It is also very open, with the only thing obstructing the view into the great room being its corner pillar or anchoring wall. This floor plan also features a front porch, which keeps the tone casual and provides warmth to the front elevation.

3 LOOKS...

A. The Shawnee (at right) has a graceful appearance that is given just a touch of formality with brick accents and multi-paned sidelights and an arched transom around the front door.

B. Because the porch is a central element on these homes, we created three elevations to celebrate its styling. The prominent windows on the McClellan (pg. 67) are given special attention with shutters and wide transoms above. The porch has a classic appeal here, framed by an entry comprised of Doric columns.

C. Flower boxes add a nice touch to the Indian Springs (pg. 68) and help balance the expanse of the porch on this elevation. The decorative columns are in tune with its simplified nature.

A. Shawnee

#48A-2461 S *Price Code* A18

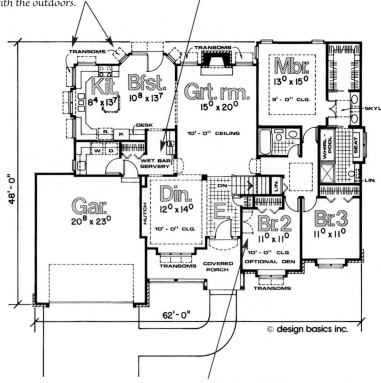

Transom windows throughout the kitchen, breakfast area and great room help integrate these areas with the outdoors.

A large wet bar/servery is located midway betwee the dining room and kitchen for easy service when entertaining.

1850 Finished SQ. FT.

Double doors off the entry show how easy it is to convert bedroom 2 into a den.

© design basics inc.

B. McClellan

#48A-5496 S *Price Code* **A19**

1924 Finished Sq. Ft.

NOTE: 9 ft. main level walls

A side-load version opens up the opportunity for storage space in the garage.

The stairway was removed from the foyer, to create an even more open view between the entry, dining room and great room.

The laundry room's location is just steps from each bedroom.

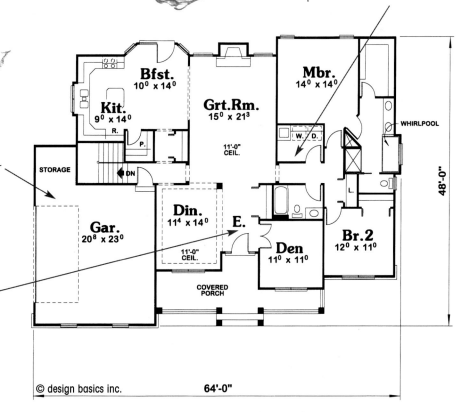

Kit. 9⁰ x 14⁰
Bfst. 10⁰ x 14⁰
Grt.Rm. 15⁰ x 21³
11'-0" CEIL.
Mbr. 14⁰ x 14⁰
WHIRLPOOL
STORAGE
DN
W. D.
L.
Gar. 20⁸ x 23⁰
Din. 11⁴ x 14⁰
11'-0" CEIL.
E.
Den 11⁰ x 11⁰
Br.2 12⁰ x 11⁰
COVERED PORCH
48'-0"
© design basics inc.
64'-0"

C. Indian Springs

1842 Finished SQ. FT.

#48A-8059 S   *Price Code* A18

A corner, soaking tub between his and her vanities resists all temptation not to relax in the master suite.

Ten-foot-high ceilings throughout all living areas of the home, inevitably create a feeling of spaciousness.

An island counter was a good choice in this kitchen because it continues the open atmosphere throughout the home.

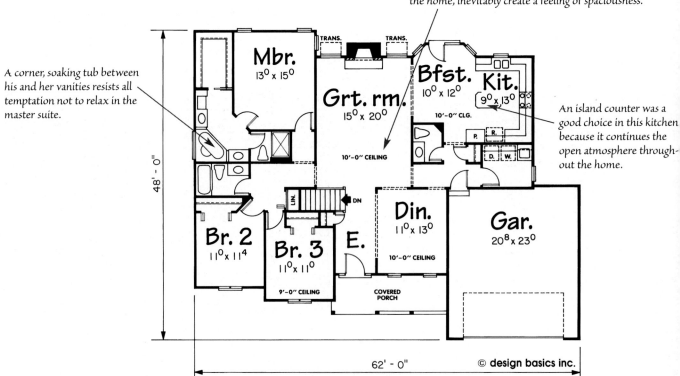

48' - 0"

62' - 0"

© design basics inc.

Mbr.
13⁰ x 15⁰

Grt. rm.
15⁰ x 20⁰
10'-0" CEILING

TRANS.   TRANS.

Bfst.
10⁰ x 12⁰
10'-0" CLG.

Kit.
9⁰ x 13⁰

Br. 2
11⁰ x 11⁴

Br. 3
11⁰ x 11⁰
9'-0" CEILING

E.

Din.
11⁰ x 13⁰
10'-0" CEILING

Gar.
20⁸ x 23⁰

COVERED PORCH

DN   LIN.

P.   R.
D.   W.

IMPRESSIONS – Homes designed with the look you wa

A. Delrose

#48A-5494 S *Price Code A26*

Main: 1916 Sq. Ft.
Second: 684 Sq. Ft.

Total: 2600 Sq. Ft.

NOTE: 9 ft. main level walls

A walk-in pantry will naturally create additional counter space in the kitchen.

© design basics inc.

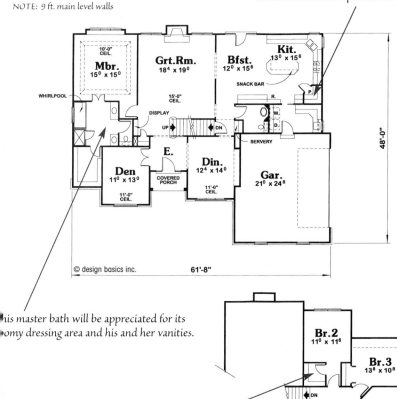

This master bath will be appreciated for its roomy dressing area and his and her vanities.

Walk-in closets on the second floor are smart for seasonal or toy storage.

A. THE DELROSE
B. THE AMBROSE
C. THE MITCHELL CREEK

ONE CONCEPT...

One of the nicest things about this design is the overall width of the great room. You can get a lot of furniture in here and, therefore, seat a lot of people for family gatherings and entertaining. The den is also a nice option in this home. It has a very secluded position on the floorplan, which is desirable for homeowners who use it as a retreat, a place to catch up on office work, or as a home office. A couple of great "extras" we provided in this home are a great light source in the kitchen through corner windows and a compartmentalized bath on the second floor to be shared by the three bedrooms.

3 LOOKS...

A. The elevation of the Delrose (at left) takes on a rather subtle approach. A facade almost completely finished in brick reveals its refinement. A dormer with a shed roof provides a unique element, but one that's in tune with the nature of its understated appeal.

B. By contrast, the entry on the Ambrose (pg. 70) is what makes the elevation appear dignified. It was meant to be noticed, which is one of the reasons we encased it in brick. All of the other elements seem to fall into place behind it - the second-level gable and multi-hipped roofline.

C. The elevation on the Mitchell Creek (pg. 71) provides an equally appealing choice for this floor plan. Brick trim fanning out as wing walls, combined with a tall central facing - it really speaks for itself.

B. *Ambrose*

Main: 1701 Sq. Ft.
Second: 639 Sq. Ft.

Total: 2340 Sq. Ft.

#48A-2701 S *Price Code* A23

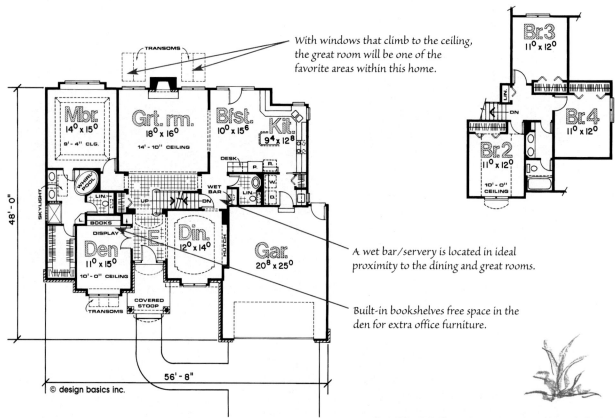

With windows that climb to the ceiling, the great room will be one of the favorite areas within this home.

TRANSOMS

Mbr.
14⁰ x 15⁰
9' - 4" CLG.

Grt. rm.
18⁰ x 16⁰
14' - 10" CEILING

Bfst.
10⁰ x 15⁶

Kit.
9⁴ x 12⁸

DESK

WHIRL POOL

LIN.

UP

DN

WET BAR

LIN.

BOOKS
DISPLAY

Den
11⁰ x 15⁰
10' - 0" CEILING

Din.
12⁰ x 14⁰

HUTCH

Gar.
20⁸ x 25⁰

SKYLIGHT

48' - 0"

COVERED STOOP

TRANSOMS

56' - 8"

© design basics inc.

Br. 3
11⁰ x 12⁰

LIN.

DN

Br. 4
11⁰ x 12⁰

Br. 2
11⁰ x 12⁰
10' - 0" CEILING

A wet bar/servery is located in ideal proximity to the dining and great rooms.

Built-in bookshelves free space in the den for extra office furniture.

C. Mitchell Creek

#48A-8042 S *Price Code* A24

The great room strikes a good balance between separation and integration with the kitchen.

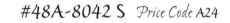

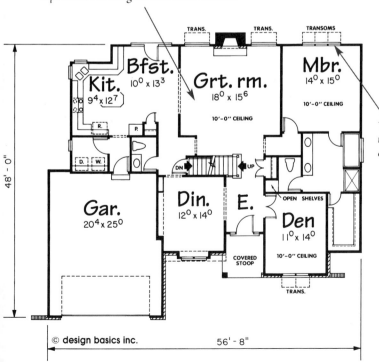

Kit. 9⁴ x 12⁷
Bfst. 10⁰ x 13³
Grt. rm. 18⁰ x 15⁶
10'-0" CEILING
Mbr. 14⁰ x 15⁰
10'-0" CEILING
TRANS. TRANS. TRANSOMS
Gar. 20⁴ x 25⁰
Din. 12⁰ x 14⁰
E.
Den 11⁰ x 14⁰
10'-0" CEILING
OPEN SHELVES
COVERED STOOP
TRANS.
DN UP
48' - 0"
56' - 8"

© design basics inc.

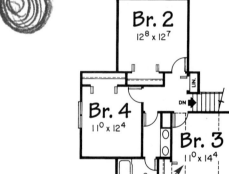

Br. 2 12⁸ x 12⁷
Br. 4 11⁰ x 12⁴
Br. 3 11⁰ x 14⁴
10'-0" CLG.
LIN.
DN

The triplet of windows in this master bedroom will be appreciated for the view they provide.

Guests will enjoy the unique design features of bedroom 3.

Main: 1717 SQ. FT.
Second: 692 SQ. FT.

Total: 2409 SQ. FT.

BUILT BY: Jerry Hermiller

#48A-2293 S *Price Code* A28

Ellison

#48A-2702 S *Price Code* A24

BUILT BY: Kahnk Homes

This covered porch will be a well-utilized area of this home with its built-in bench and space for patio furniture.

The master suite is much more of a retreat with private access to a den.

This home was definitely meant for a family, with dual stairway offering formal and informal access to the second level.

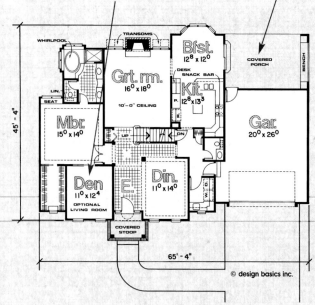

© design basics inc.

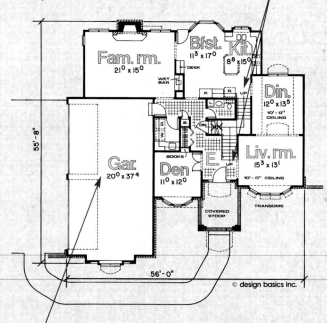

© design basics inc.

A four-car garage leaves plenty of room for a workspace and storage.

Immediately when you walk in, you can't help but be impressed with the two-story entry viewing a second-level balcony.

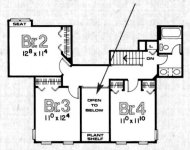

A great addition to the master suite is its bayed sitting area. What a won-derful place to read the morning paper and enjoy a cup of coffee!

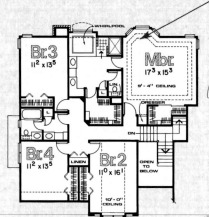

Main: 1716 Sq. Ft.
Second: 716 Sq. Ft.

Total: 2432 Sq. Ft.

Main: 1501 Sq. Ft.
Second: 1389 Sq. Ft.

Total: 2890 Sq. Ft.

IMPRESSIONS- *Homes designed with the look you wa*

BUILT BY: Falcone Enterprises

BUILT BY: Dale Yost Construction

Baldwin

#48A-2962 S *Price Code* A23

The T-shaped staircase is a convenient way to direct traffic to the second level.

The laundry room has excellent features, such as a soaking sink, large closet and built-in ironing board.

A pair of bookshelves in the family room is a great place for books and family photos.

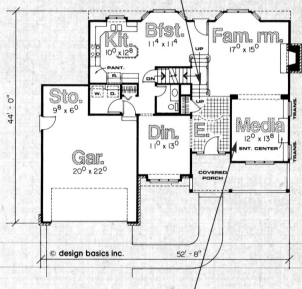

© design basics inc.

© design basics inc.

The separate media room is a great place for children to go when having guests over.

On the second level, a pocket door separates the master suite into a secluded wing. A balcony, double doors, walk-in closet and corner whirlpool tub are among the features to enjoy in privacy.

Many will take advantage of this long, wrap-around porch.

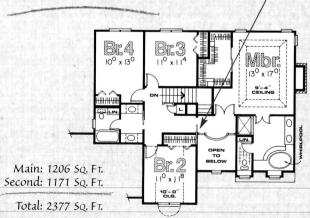

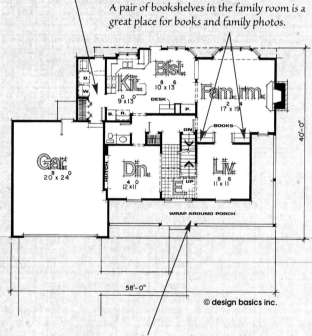

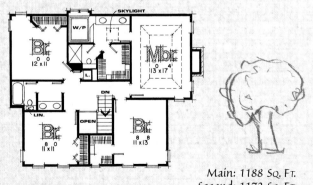

Main: 1206 Sq. Ft.
Second: 1171 Sq. Ft.

Total: 2377 Sq. Ft.

Main: 1188 Sq. Ft.
Second: 1172 Sq. Ft.

Total: 2360 Sq. Ft.

DESIGN TRIO #17

A. THE COLUMBUS
B. THE PATAGONIA
C. THE BENTLEY WOODS

ONE CONCEPT...

The main living area in this floor plan is what makes this home unique. It is located just inside the entry and is designed to serve both formally and informally. It's location across from the dining room makes it perfect on formal occasions and its open access to the kitchen still allows it connection for everyday living. A charming aspect of this home is a covered porch off the breakfast area. It serves as a place to get away or it can be used to cook or enjoy a meal outdoors.

3 LOOKS...

A. The exterior of the Columbus (at right) comes directly from Georgian styling with a straight face, the only protrusion being the front entry. This classic styling looks great anywhere it is built.

B. The all-stucco exterior of the Patagonia (pg. 75) really gives it distinction. The addition of dormers over the garage and a double gable over the entry create opposite focal points for exterior appeal.

C. The Bentley Woods (pg. 75) has a more traditional feel with the inclusion of a front porch. It has a more unique look due to its gable and hip roof combination.

A. Columbus

#48A-2963 S *Price Code A19*

Main: 941 SQ. FT.
Second: 992 SQ. FT.

Total: 1933 SQ. FT.

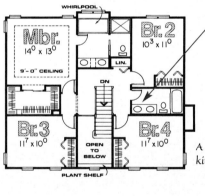

The double vanity in the second-floor bath is a thoughtful feature to be shared by three bedrooms

The kitchen and breakfast area are integrated and really function as a single unit for everyday living.

A service counter aids the kitchen in serving formal meals.

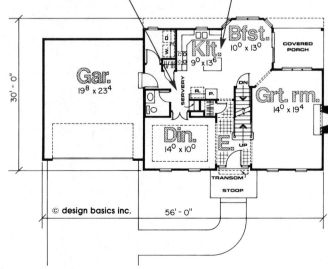

© design basics inc.

B. *Patagonia*

#48A-5086 S *Price Code* A24

A second-floor laundry room makes sense in this design.
A long dormer providing light is a quaint touch.

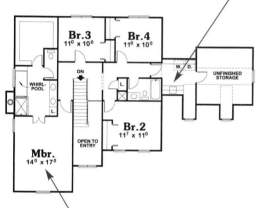

This master suite is ideally secluded from the
three other bedrooms on the second level.

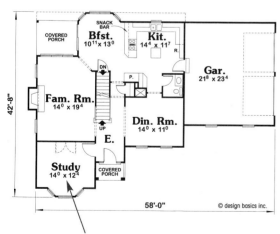

The addition of a study to this home creates
a quiet place for homework or office work.

Main: 1162 Sq. Ft.
Second: 1255 Sq. Ft.

Total: 2417 Sq. Ft.

NOTE: 9 ft. main level walls

C. *Bentley Woods*

#48A-8082 S *Price Code* A19

A pair of dormers will give atmosphere to whatever
use is made of this second-floor bonus room.

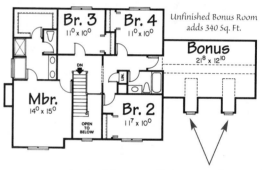

Windows on two sides of the breakfast area will make
it feel larger than it is.

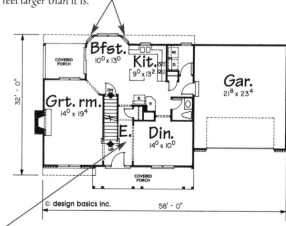

The two-story entry immediately makes
this home feel open and spacious.

Main: 945 Sq. Ft.
Second: 1007 Sq. Ft.

Total: 1952 Sq. Ft.

HOME OWNER IMPRESSIONS
ON LIVING IN THE TIMBER POINT

Lori is not a superstitious person, but neither does she like to test fate. She didn't realize until just before she and her husband Barry closed on their new home, that their house number would be 13.

"Who would ever number a house 13? The number is usually eliminated in apartment buildings and office floors," she says jokingly.

So far the seemingly unlucky number has not unleashed any side effects. In fact, their home, Design Basics Timber Point, couldn't be a better fit for Barry, Lori and their two teenage daughters.

It was over a year ago when the time came for them to look for a new home. And when they came across the Timber Point, a home built on speculation in their area, they knew almost immediately they liked what they saw.

"I think the thing that attracted us right away was the kitchen," Barry says.

"The thing that makes it so nice is the spaciousness. It has an island counter, lots of counter space and a nice eating area. There's lots of space to have conversation. It just seems like we're always hanging out in there."

The family of four also appreciates the location of the bedrooms in the Timber Point. "It came as a nice surprise that the master suite was located on the main floor," Lori says. "Now the girls can go upstairs on the other side of the home and we aren't bothered by their

continued on page 78

Openness was created in the kitchen without sacrificing built-in storage space.

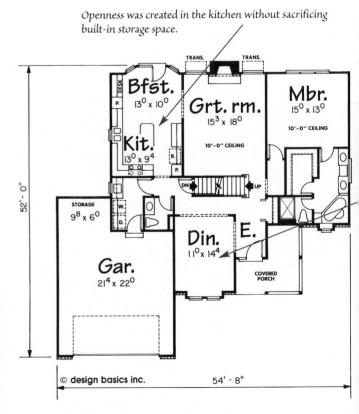

Bfst. 13⁰ x 10⁰

Grt. rm. 15³ x 18⁰
10'-0" CEILING

Mbr. 15⁰ x 13⁰
10'-0" CEILING

Kit. 13⁰ x 9⁴

DESK

TRANS.   TRANS.

STORAGE 9⁸ x 6⁰

DN   UP

Din. 11⁰ x 14⁴

E.

Gar. 21⁴ x 22⁰

COVERED PORCH

52'- 0"

© design basics inc.   54'- 8"

IMPRESSIONS– *Homes designed with the look you wa*

ONE CONCEPT...

A variety of inherent traits make this floor plan ideal. It features a formal entry that focuses exclusively on the dining room, along with a directed path to the kitchen. This pathway recesses the great room and thus sets up its more informal function within the home. A lavish master bath centers on a soaking tub or whirlpool - whichever you choose - to create the ultimate place to de-stress. A large storage area located in the garage is also an aspect of this design that will neither be overlooked, nor unwelcome.

3 LOOKS...

A *The Timber Point's (at left) tidy front elevation is dressed up with brick accents and an eye-catching front porch that's reminiscent of picket fencing.*

B *A central aspect of the Eldorado (pg. 78) is its angled front porch distinguishing both the entry and elevation.*

C *Since the triple windows make up the elemental design of the Camrose's (pg. 79) facade, this home will be appealing whether finished completely in brick, siding or with a mixture, as shown here.*

A. Timber Point

#48A-8075 S   *Price Code* A19

The extension of the dining rom in this design is not only a striking visual element, but it also offers a bit of extra room for seating guests.

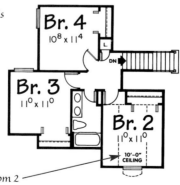

A 10-foot ceiling and arched window in bedroom 2 will only enhance its interior decorating.

Main: 1426 SQ. FT.
Second: 568 SQ. FT.

Total: 1994 SQ. FT.

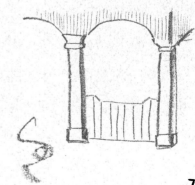

music or TV. And I think for them it's nice because at their age, they want some privacy."

But perhaps more appreciated than the separation of the bedrooms is the fact that Barry and Lori enjoy a separate bath in the master suite. In their previous home, the family shared one main bath.

As a result, the master bath is another favorite place within the home. The dual-sink vanity allows both Barry and Lori the designated space they need in the morning. Lori takes advantage of the corner soaking tub to unwind. And because their walk-in closet is located in the master bath, each can get ready without having to wake the other.

Though the home isn't much bigger than their previous home, both Barry and Lori say it feels much more open and spacious because of the tall ceilings and the integration of the living areas. "When you walk in the front door, it is wide open. You have a view of the oak staircase and the dining room. But there are no walls that separate anything. There's a lot of airiness inside."

Since there isn't much Barry and Lori can do about changing their home's destiny with the number 13, their house number and address remain the same. But just to be on the safe side...

"I found the tiniest number one and three that they sold in the store and put them on the mailbox. It's nowhere on the house itself!" Lori admits, laughing.

B. Eldorado

#48A- 2719 S Price Code A19

Tall windows in the great room and breakfast area were designed to dramatize the slope of their 10-foot-high ceilings.

Br.4 10⁷ x 11⁴

OPEN TO GREAT ROOM

DN

Br.3 11⁰ x 11⁰

OPEN TO BELOW

Br.2 11⁰ x 11⁰

TRANSOMS   TRANSOMS

Mbr. 15⁰ x 13⁰ 10'-0" CEILING

Grt. rm. 15³ x 18⁰ SLOPED CEILING

Bfst. 13⁰ x 11⁰ 10'-0" CEILING SNACK BAR

Kit. 13⁰ x 11⁷

This kitchen provides a snack bar for those who prefer a place for a quick meal.

Sto. 9⁰ x 10⁰

51' - 8"

TRANSOM

LIN.

WHIRLPOOL

UP   DN

COVERED PORCH

Din. 11⁰ x 13⁴

Gar. 20⁸ x 22⁰

A bay of windows with accenting plant shelf, helps emphasize this two-story entry.

54' - 0"

© design basics inc.

Main: 1413 Sq. Ft.
Second: 563 Sq. Ft.

Total: 1976 Sq. Ft.

IMPRESSIONS- Homes designed with the look you wa

C. Camrose

#48A-5149 S *Price Code* A21

The inclusion of a library – complete with built-in bookshelves – establishes the old-world feel one garners from its exterior.

A side-load garage easily fits into the core design of this home.

Main: 1624 SQ. FT.
Second: 566 SQ. FT.

Total: 2190 SQ. FT.

NOTE: 9 ft. main level walls

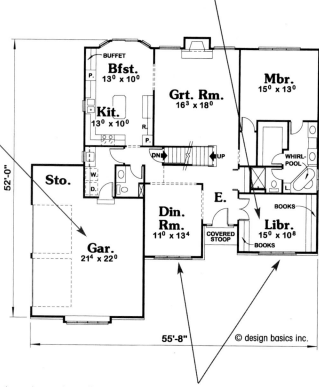

Triple-wide windows illuminate both the interior and exterior of this home.

© design basics inc.

Albany

#48A-2235 S *Price Code* A19

One of the most enjoyable aspects of this great room will be the amount of light brought in by front and rear windows with transoms above.

With such dramatic windows lining every room located to the back, this home was surely meant for a lot with a view.

Plenty of storage in the garage allows space for a work center and bike and equipment storage.

Beautiful dome ceilings are repeated throughout this design in the breakfast area, master bath and stairway.

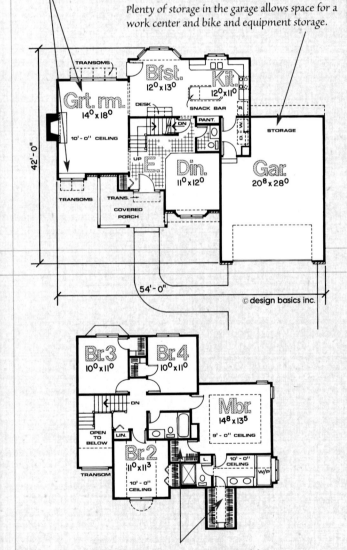

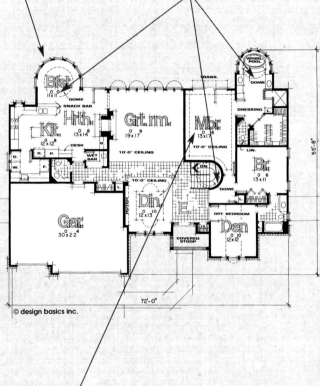

His and her walk-in closets are a wonderful feature in the master suite.

A curved wall, walk-in closet with his and her compartments and shower trimmed in glass block are memorable aspects of the master suite.

2422 Finished Sq. Ft.

Main: 944 Sq. Ft.
Second: 987 Sq. Ft.

Total: 1931 Sq. Ft.

IMPRESSIONS- *Homes designed with the look you w*

Auburn

48A-5161 S *Price Code* A21

A second closet in the master suite is great for extra bedding or seasonal clothing storage.

A snack bar provides additional seating in the breakfast area.

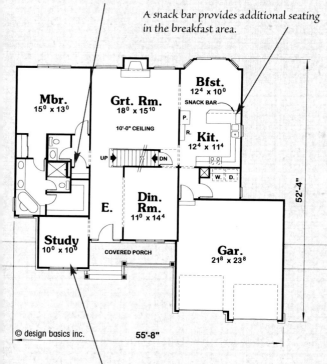

The location of the study makes it a great place to work, or just to get away from activity.

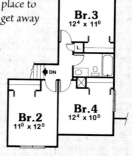

Main: 1569 SQ. FT.
Second: 598 SQ. FT.

Total: 2167 SQ. FT.

NOTE: 9 ft. main level walls

Thrifton

#48A-3441 S *Price Code* A23

A triple display gallery makes an eye-catching view whether just entering the home or entertaining in the formal rooms.

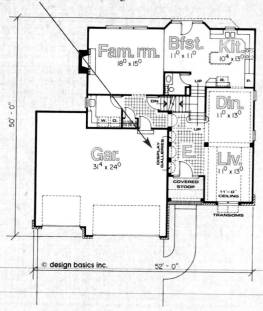

Even though there are many pampering features in the master bath, its spaciousness will be the most appreciated.

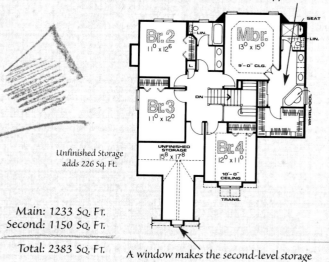

Unfinished Storage adds 226 SQ. Ft.

Main: 1233 SQ. FT.
Second: 1150 SQ. FT.

Total: 2383 SQ. FT.

A window makes the second-level storage area more functional.

Design Trio #19

A. The Pinehurst
B. The Crescent Creek
C. The Middleboro

One Concept...

This floor plan has a lot of advantages to it. It has a great family area at the back of the home that's quite separated from the other areas. The central hall of this home is comprised of a formal living and dining room. This area is so nicely separated that you could actually have entertaining going on in two areas of the home. The master suite is also located on the main floor, which offers great separation from the children. A lavish bath is attached for real relaxation at the end of the day. And to top it all off, it features a den that could become a home office.

3 Looks...

A. The Pinehurst (at right) has an impressive grace to it with its brick exterior, copper eave and upscale entry. It seems to have roots in neo-French styling.

B. The Crescent Creek's elevation (pg. 83) takes on a traditional feel that has a welcoming aspect to it. Its brick detail dresses it up enough to make it a little bit dignified, so it is really versatile for any neighborhood.

C. The sheer size of the Middleboro (pg. 83) will make it feel as impressive as it is. But it is nevertheless unpretentious with the accent of batten-board shutters, a front porch and an array of windows on the exterior.

A. Pinehurst

#48A-2311 S Price Code A

Main: 1829 Sq. Ft.
Second: 657 Sq. Ft.

Total: 2486 Sq. Ft.

A unique angle in the breakfast area floods it with light and creates visual separation from the gathering room.

Bayed windows wrap the whirlpool tub in light and luxury.

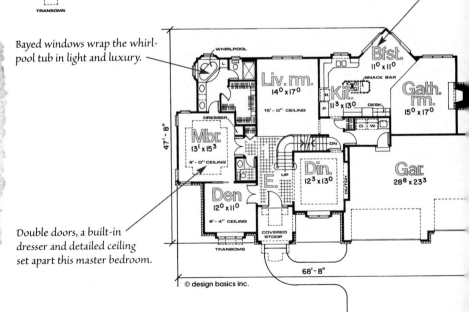

Double doors, a built-in dresser and detailed ceiling set apart this master bedroom.

© design basics inc.

IMPRESSIONS– *Homes designed with the look you w...*

B. *Crescent Creek*

#48A-8127 S *Price Code* A25

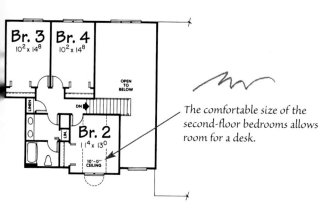

Br. 3
10² x 14⁸

Br. 4
10² x 14⁸

OPEN TO BELOW

LINEN

DN

Br. 2
11⁴ x 13⁰

LIN.

10'-0" CEILING

The comfortable size of the second-floor bedrooms allows room for a desk.

The kitchen, breakfast area and family room function as one room and create a natural area for family to convene.

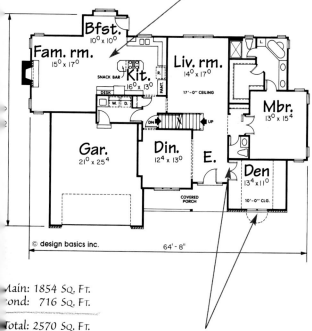

Bfst.
10⁰ x 10⁰

Fam. rm.
15⁰ x 17⁰

SNACK BAR

Kit.
16⁰ x 13⁰

PANT.

Liv. rm.
14⁰ x 17⁰

17'-0" CEILING

DESK

W. D.

Mbr.
13⁰ x 15⁴

Gar.
21⁰ x 25⁴

DN

UP

Din.
12⁴ x 13⁰

E.

Den
13⁴ x11⁰

10'-0" CLG.

COVERED PORCH

© design basics inc.

64'- 8"

Main: 1854 Sq. Ft.
Second: 716 Sq. Ft.

Total: 2570 Sq. Ft.

Double doors and an arched window create a stimulating atmosphere in the den.

C. *Middleboro*

#48A-5000 S *Price Code* A29

This master suite is provided a rear view to take advantage of a waterfront or golf course.

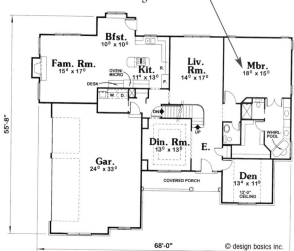

55'-8"

Bfst.
10⁰ x 10⁰

Fam. Rm.
15⁴ x 17⁰

OVEN/MICRO

Kit.
11⁴ x 13⁰

R.

DESK

W. D.

Liv. Rm.
14⁰ x 17⁰

Mbr.
18⁰ x 15⁰

DN

UP

Din. Rm.
13⁰ x 13⁰

E.

WHIRL-POOL

Gar.
24⁰ x 33⁰

COVERED PORCH

Den
13⁴ x 11⁰

12'-0" CEILING

68'-0"

© design basics inc.

This storage area has possibilities ranging from a finished room to storage closet.

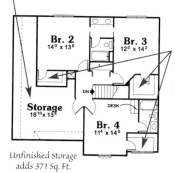

Br. 2
14⁰ x 13⁶

Br. 3
12⁰ x 14²

DN

DESK

Storage
18¹⁰ x 13⁴

Br. 4
11⁴ x 14⁰

Even more storage is provided in three walk-in closets that accompany the second-floor bedrooms.

Unfinished Storage adds 371 Sq. Ft.

Main: 2072 Sq. Ft.
Second: 917 Sq. Ft.

Total: 2989 Sq. Ft.

NOTE: 10 ft. main level walls

BUILT BY: Focus Homes Inc.

Bennington

#48A-1855 S *Price Code* A23

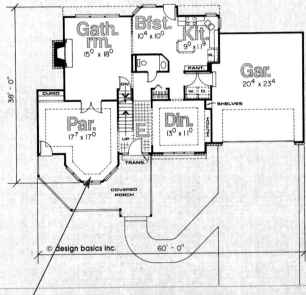

One of the things I enjoy most about this home is the parlor. The bayed windows give it an open, airy feel and it has access to the front porch.

A feature that might get missed on the second level is this handy clothes chute.

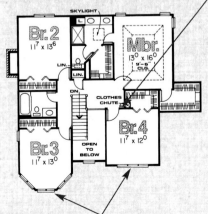

Beautiful windows make bedrooms 3 and 4 stand out.

Main: 1183 Sq. Ft.
Second: 1209 Sq. Ft.

Total: 2392 Sq. Ft.

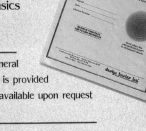
IMPRESSIONS – Homes designed with the look you w

CUSTOMIZED PLAN CHANGES

PRICE SCHEDULE

ALL PLANS *Customizable*

2 X 6 EXTERIOR WALLS .... $175 .....
FROM STANDARD 2 X 4 TO 2 X 6 EXTERIOR WALLS

EACH GARAGE ALTERATION .... $325 .....
  • FRONT-ENTRY TO SIDE LOAD (OR VICE VERSA)
  • 2-CAR TO 3-CAR (OR VICE VERSA)
  • 2-CAR FRONT-ENTRY TO 3-CAR SIDE -LOAD (OR VICE VERSA)
  • 3-CAR FRONT-ENTRY TO 2-CAR SIDE -LOAD (OR VICE VERSA)

WALK-OUT BASEMENT.. $195 .....

CRAWL SPACE FOUNDATION .... $250 .....

SLAB FOUNDATION .... $250 .....

STRETCH CHANGES .... $6 per lineal foot of cut

ADDITIONAL BRICK TO SIDES & REAR .... $350 .....

ADDITIONAL BRICK TO FRONT,
  SIDES AND REAR .... $450 .....

ALTERNATE PRELIMINARY ELEVATION .... $195 .....

9-FOOT MAIN LEVEL WALLS .... starting at $195

SPECIFY WINDOW BRAND (WITHOUT OTHER CHANGES - $150) .... $95 .....

POURED CONCRETE FOUNDATION
ONLY WITH OTHER CHANGES (WITHOUT OTHER CHANGES - $150) .... $25 .....

ADDING ONE COURSE (8") TO THE FOUNDATION HEIGHT
ONLY WITH OTHER CHANGES (WITHOUT OTHER CHANGES - $150) .... $25 .....

NOTE ··

  • All plan changes come to you on erasable, reproducible vellums.
  • An unchanged set of original vellums is available for only $50 along with your plan changes.
  • Design Basics changes are not made to the artist's renderings, electrical, sections or cabinets.
  • Prices are subject to change.

As a part of our commitment to help you achieve the "perfect" home, we offer an extensive variety of plan changes for any Design Basics plan. For those whose decision to purchase a home plan is contingent upon the feasibility of a plan change, our Customer Support Specialists will, in most cases, be able to provide a FREE price quote for the changes.

call us toll-free at

(800) 947-7526

to order plan changes listed here, or if you have questions regarding plan changes not listed.

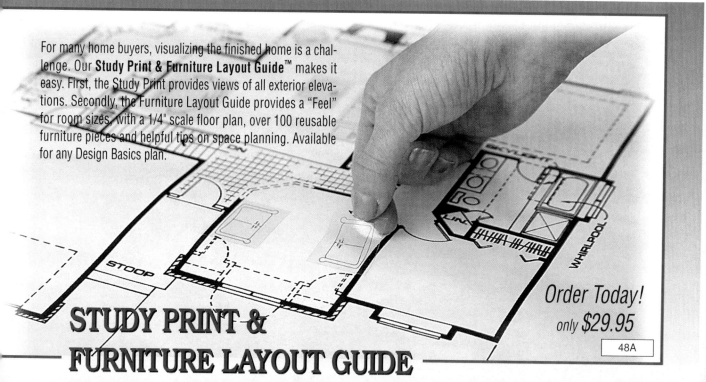

For many home buyers, visualizing the finished home is a challenge. Our **Study Print & Furniture Layout Guide**™ makes it easy. First, the Study Print provides views of all exterior elevations. Secondly, the Furniture Layout Guide provides a "Feel" for room sizes, with a 1/4" scale floor plan, over 100 reusable furniture pieces and helpful tips on space planning. Available for any Design Basics plan.

Order Today!
only $29.95

48A

STUDY PRINT & FURNITURE LAYOUT GUIDE

DESIGN BASICS' HOME PLAN LIBRARY

Easy Living One-Story Designs™ – 155 one-story home ...igns from the Gold Seal™, Heartland Home Plans™ and ...meless Legacy™ collections, together in one plan book. $7.95

Timeless Legacy™, A Collection of Fine Home ...igns by Carmichael & Dame – 52 breathtaking luxury ...ue designs from 3300' to 4500'. Includes artful rear views of ... home. $25.00

The Narrow Home™ Collection – 258 one-story, 1 ½ story ... 2-story home plans that are from 26 to 50 feet wide. Many ... be joined together to create customized duplex plans. $14.95

Heartland Home Plans™ – 120 plan ideas designed for ...yday practicality. Warm, unpretentious elevations easily ...pt to individual lifestyles. From 1212' to 2631'. $8.95

On the Porch™ – A Designer's Journal of Notes and ...ches – 64 designs from Gold Seal™, Heartland Home ...s™ and Timeless Legacy™ – each one with a porch. Includes ... on the porch and it's role in traditional design. $2.95

6) Gold Seal™ Home Plan Book Set – 442 of today's most sought-after one-story, 1 ½ story and 2-story home plan ideas.
All 5 books for $84.95 or $19.95 each
• Homes of Distinction – 86 plans under 1800'
• Homes of Sophistication – 106 plans, 1800'-2199'
• Homes of Elegance – 107 plans, 2200'-2599'
• Homes of Prominence – 75 plans, 2600'-2999'
• Homes of Grandeur – 68 plans, 3000'-4000'

7) Gold Seal Favorites™ – 100 best selling plans from the famous Gold Seal™ Collection, including 25 duplex designs. $6.95

8) Nostalgia Home Plans Collection™ – A New Approach to Time-Honored Design – 70 designs showcasing enchanting details and unique "special places." From 1339' to 3480'. $9.95

9) Nostalgia Home Plans Collection™ Vol. II – A New Approach to Time-Honored Design – 70 designs bringing back the essence of homes of the past. $9.95

10) Photographed Portraits of an American Home™ – 100 of our finest designs, beautifully photographed and tastefully presented among charming photo album memories of "home". A must for any sales center's coffee table. $14.95

11) Reflections of an American Home™ Vol. III – 50 photographed home plans with warm remembrances of home and beautiful interior presentations. From 1341' to 3775'. $4.95

12) Seasons of Life™ – Designs for Reaping the Rewards of Autumn – 100 home plans specially tailored to today's empty-nester. From 1212' to 3904'. $4.95

13) Seasons of Life™ – Designs for Living Summer's Journey – 100 designs from, 1605' to 3775' for the move-up buyer. $4.95

14) Seasons of Life™ – Designs for Spring's New Beginnings – 100 home plans for first-time buyers. Presentations unique to this lifestyle. From 1125' to 2537'. $4.95

Order the complete Seasons of Life™ set (all three books) for only $9.00

A Plan From Design Basics: What's In It For You?

Plans come to you on high-quality reproducible vellums and include the following:

1. **Cover Page.** Each Design Basics home plan features the rendered elevation and informative reference sections including: general notes and design criteria;* abbreviations; and symbols for your Design Basics' plan.

2. **Elevations.** Drafted at ¼" scale for the front and ⅛" scale for the rear and sides. All elevations are detailed and an aerial view of the roof is provided, showing all hips, valleys and ridges.

3. **Foundations.** Drafted at ¼" scale. Block foundations and basements are standard. We also show the HVAC equipment, structural information,* steel beam and pole locations and the direction and spacing of the floor system above.

4. **Main Level Floor Plan.** ¼" scale. Fully dimensioned from stud to stud for ease of framing. 2"x4" walls are standard. The detailed drawings include such things as structural header locations, framing layout and kitchen layout.

5. **Second Level Floor Plan.** ¼" scale. Dimensioned from stud to stud and drafted to the same degree of detail as the main level floor plan.*

6. **Interior Elevations.** Useful for the cabinet and bidding process, this page shows all kitchen and bathroom cabinets as well as any other cabinet elevations.

7. **Electrical and Sections.** Illustrated on a separate page for clarity, the electrical plan shows suggested electrical layout for the foundation, main and second level floor plans. Typical wall, cantilever, stair, brick and fireplace sections are provided to further explain construction of these areas.

All plan orders received prior to 2:00 p.m. CT will be processed, inspected and shipped out the same afternoon via 2n ness day air within the continental United All other product orders will be sent v ground service. Full Technical Support is av for any plan purchase from Design Basic Technical Support Specialists provide unl technical support free of charge and answer qu regarding construction methods, framing techniqu more. Please call 800-947-7526 for more information.

CONSTRUCTION LICENSE

When you purchase a Design Basics home plan, you rec Construction License which gives you certain rights in building the depicted in that plan, including:

No Re-Use Fee. As the original purchaser of a Design Basics home plan, the Cons License permits you to build the plan as many times as you like.

Local Modifications. The Construction License allows you to make modifications Design Basics plans. We offer a complete custom change service, or you may h desired changes done locally by a qualified draftsman, designer, architect or enginee

Running Blueprints. Your plans are sent to you on vellum paper that reproduces your blueprint machine. The Construction License authorizes you or your blueprint at your direction, to make as many copies of the plan from the vellum masters as y for construction purposes.

* Our plans are drafted to meet average conditions and codes in the state of Nebraska, at the time they are designed. Because codes and requirements can change and may vary from jurisdiction to jurisdiction, Design Basics Inc. cannot warrant compliance with any specific regulation. All Design Basics plans can be adapted to your local building codes and requirements. It is the responsibility of the purchaser and/or builder of each plan to see that the structure is built in strict compliance with all governing municipal codes (city, county, state and

---

TO ORDER DIRECT: CALL 800-947-7526 ASK FOR DEPT. 48A · MONDAY – FRIDAY 7:00 a.m. – 6:00 p.m. CST

Name _____   Company _____

Address _____   Title _____
(For UPS Delivery – Packages cannot be shipped to a P.O. Box.)

Above Address: ☐ business address ☐ residence address   City _____ State _____ Zip _____

☐ Visa [VISA] ☐ AMEX   Credit Card: Phone ( ) _____ FAX ( ) _____

☐ MasterCard [MasterCard] ☐ Discover [DISCOVER]   Expiration Date: [ ][ ] / [ ][ ]

☐ Check enclosed (All orders payable in U.S. funds only)

Signature _____

✓	HOME PLAN PRODUCTS	PLAN #	QTY.	PRICE	SHIPPING & HANDLING	TOTAL
☐	1 Complete Set of Master Reproducible/Modifiable Vellum Prints				2nd Day Air at No Charge	$
☐	Add'l. Sets of Blueprints - $20.00 Plan #9114-#9121-#9160-#9167-#9168-#9169 – $40.00				$4.95 or No Charge if Shipped with plan	$
☐	Add'l. Sets of Mirror Reverse Blueprints - $20.00 Plan #9114-#9121-#9160-#9167-#9168-#9169 – $40.00				$4.95 or No Charge if Shipped with plan	$
☐	Materials & Estimator's Workbook - $50.00 (Not Available for plans #9114-#9121-#9160-#9167-#9168-#9169-#24002-#24004-#24005)				$4.95 or No Charge if Shipped with plan	$
☐	Study Print & Furniture Layout Guide–$29.95 *Study print for #9114-#9121-#9160-#9167-#9168-#9169 – $25 (Not Available for plans #24002-#24004 and #24005)				$4.95	$
☐	RoomScapes™ Layout Guide - $29.95 (Not Available for plans #9114-#9121-#9160-#9167-#9168-#9169-#24002-#24004-#24005)				$4.95	$
☐	Impressions of Home™- Homes Designed With the Look You Want–$4.95				$4.95	$
☐	Plan Book Deal – $100.00				$4.95	$

BOOK NUMBER	BOOK NAME		
		1 or More Plan Books $4.95	$
			$

• All Design Basics plans come with a basement foundation. • Alternate foundations available through our Custom Change Dept.
• Shipping prices for Continental U.S. only • No refunds or exchanges, please.

All COD's must be paid by Certified Check, Cashier's Check or Money Order.
(Additional $10.00 charge on COD Orders) — $ 10.00

CALL 800-947-7526
ASK FOR DEPT. 48A
OR MAIL ORDER TO: **Design Basics**
11112 John Galt Blvd.
Omaha, NE 68137

Subtotal — $

TX Res. Add 6.25% Tax (on #9114-#9121-#9160-#9167-#9168 & #9169 only)
NE Residents Add 6% Sales Tax — $

Total — $

PRICES SUBJECT TO CHANGE

PLAN PRICE SCHEDULE
FOR ONE SET OF MASTER VELLUMS

Plan Price Code	Total Sq. Ft.	A
13	1300' - 1399'	$465
14	1400' - 1499'	$475
15	1500' - 1599'	$485
16	1600' - 1699'	$495
17	1700' - 1799'	$505
18	1800' - 1899'	$515
19	1900' - 1999'	$525
20	2000' - 2099'	$535
21	2100' - 2199'	$545
22	2200' - 2299'	$555
23	2300' - 2399'	$565
24	2400' - 2499'	$575
25	2500' - 2599'	$585
26	2500' - 2599'	$595
27	2500' - 2599'	$605
28	2500' - 2599'	$615
29	2500' - 2599'	$625
30	2500' - 2599'	$635
32	2500' - 2599'	$655
33	2500' - 2599'	—
34	2500' - 2599'	$675
35	2500' - 2599'	$685
39	2500' - 2599'	$725
41	2500' - 2599'	—

IMPRESSIONS of home™

When most of us imagine home in our minds, what we most certainly see first is its exterior. This view encapsulates it, often setting the tone and atmosphere of its presence. While a home is much more than its elevation, its look and style are still, undoubtedly, important. And for each of us, it should say something about who we are. IMPRESSIONS of home™ - *Homes Designed With The Look You Want*, was developed to help you find the right style and character for your home. Inside, 19 design "trios" showcase designs with three unique elevation styles and floor plan options so you can be sure that what characterizes you will not have to be sacrificed to get the home you are looking for. Insight into each of these design trios is offered from either the designers who created the floor plans or the homeowners who've lived in them. A wide variety of other floor plans are included, creating a compilation of 100 plans ranging in square footage from 1339' to 4139'. It's all about discovering the look that's right for you. IMPRESSIONS of home™ - *Homes Designed With The Look You Want* is devoted to aid you in your search and eventual discovery.

HOMES DESIGNED WITH THE LOOK YOU WANT

DESIGN BASICS ♄ *"Bringing People Home"*

design basics inc
HOME PLAN DESIGN SERVICE

IN CANADA
$ 7.9?

UPC

6 59746 07699 4

EAN
ISBN 1-892150-11-?
50495

9 781892 150110